TRUE CRIME CASE HISTORIES

VOLUME 3

JASON NEAL

AKAMAI PUBLISHING

Cover photos of:

Larry Gene Bell (top-left)

Jessica Wongso (top-right)

John Sweeney (bottom-left)

John Tanner (bottom-right)

More books by Jason Neal

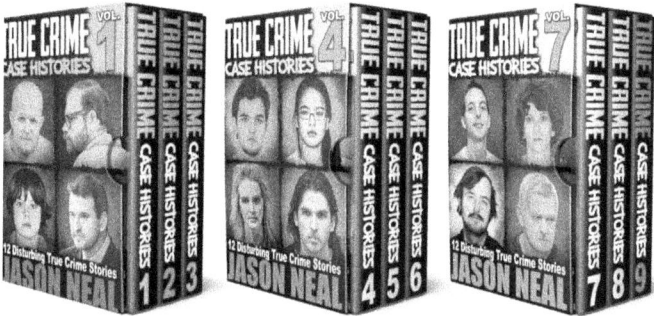

Looking for more?? I am constantly adding new volumes of True Crime Case Histories. The series **can be read in any order**, and all books are available in paperback, hardcover, and audiobook.

Check out the complete series at:

https://amazon.com/author/jason-neal

or

http://jasonnealbooks.com

All Jason Neal books are also available in **AudioBook format at Audible.com.** Enjoy a **Free Audiobook** when you signup for a 30-Day trial using this link:

https://geni.us/AudibleTrueCrime

FREE BONUS EBOOK FOR MY READERS

As my way of saying "Thank you" for downloading, I'm giving away a FREE True Crime e-book I think you'll enjoy.

https://TrueCrimeCaseHistories.com

Just visit the link above to let me know where to send your free book!

CONTENTS

INTRODUCTION

As with the two prior volumes of True Crime Case Histories, I want to start with a quick word of warning. Most news articles and television true crime shows skim over the sticky details of truly gruesome crimes. I don't gloss over the facts in my books, regardless of how horrible they may be. I try to give my readers a clear and accurate description of just how demented the killers really were. I do my best not to leave anything out. The stories included in these books are not for the squeamish.

I had read about some stories in this volume in the past, but it wasn't until I thoroughly researched the cases, reading through court documents and searching old newspaper articles, that I fully realized how disturbing they were.

I didn't intend to give this volume a theme, but it coincidentally turned out that six murders in this book involved dismemberment. In five of those murders, investigators never found some of the body parts.

There's the story of the psychopath that cut off the hands, feet, and heads of his girlfriends and dumped them in the canals of London and Rotterdam. Then, there's the drug kingpin that chopped off the head of one of his dealers and carried it around in a Home Depot bucket.

Another drug dealer butchered an entire family so he could take over a man's fruit shipping business and transform it into a drug shipping business.

There's also the story of the young woman, jealous of her wealthy socialite friend, that poisoned her by lacing her coffee with cyanide.

That's just a small sample of the twelve stories included in this book. Also, I've included a bonus chapter from a previous volume of True Crime Case Histories at the end of this book.

In many cases, I like to include what happened after the sentencing. Most of the time, the killer is caught, locked up for life, and that's the end. However, sometimes there's more to the story – whether it be something that happened while they were in prison or additional murders they're suspected of. But I'm particularly amazed at how many killers are released early, despite their horrible crimes.

In one story in this volume, I write about a woman that shot her husband, froze his body, hacked him up with a jigsaw, and was caught dumping his torso in a trash dumpster. She was released fourteen years after her conviction and is now living in France.

Another story recounts the case of a young man who strangled his girlfriend and crammed her body into an eight-inch crawlspace beneath the stairs. After serving only eleven years in jail, he was released… only to strangle his next girlfriend.

If there's any common thread between these cases, it would be that many of them happened near places I've lived throughout my life.

Three stories took place in the London area, one of which happened just a five-minute walk from my home. Two other stories took place in Scottsdale, Arizona, where I've lived a large part of my life. Another took place in Maui, Hawaii, while I was living there, and finally, another took place in Oxford, UK, very close to where I've been working over the past year.

The stories in this volume are dark and disturbing, took place all over the world, and range from the 1940s to 2018.

The stories are a bit longer this time than in the previous volumes. As usual, I've added an online appendix with more photos, videos, and documents about the cases. Look for the link at the end of the book.

Lastly, please join my mailing list for discounts, updates, and a free book. You can sign up for that at

TrueCrimeCaseHistories.com

You can also purchase paperbacks, hardcovers, and signed copies of my books directly from me at:

JasonNealBooks.com

Additional photos, videos, and documents about the cases in this volume can be found on the accompanying web page listed at the end of this book.

Thank you for reading. I sincerely hope you gain some insight from this volume of True Crime Case Histories.

- Jason

CHAPTER 1
THE COFFEE KILLER

The Billy Blue College of Design was nestled beneath the Harbor Bridge in Sydney, Australia. Sydney was a long way from Indonesia, which was perhaps why Mirna Salihin and Jessica Wongso became such close friends. They had both started their first year at the prestigious school for graphic design, and they had both come from Jakarta, Indonesia, specifically to attend the school.

The young girls were like two peas in a pod. Both came from wealthy Indonesian families, had a passion for graphic design, and were eager to start their careers. They were inseparable.

After graduation from college, however, Mirna took a job in Jakarta, where her family still lived, while Jessica stayed in Sydney. Jessica loved Sydney so much that her parents and two siblings also immigrated there in 2008.

Jessica Wongso & Mirna Salihin

As the years went by, Jessica and Mirna kept in touch. Both had secured well-paying jobs doing graphic design and had fallen in love with young men: Mirna with a young Indonesian man, and Jessica with a young Australian man. However, the men differed significantly from each other.

In 2014, when Mirna took a vacation back to Sydney, the two girls met to catch up. During their time together, Mirna and Jessica discussed their lives, work, and boyfriends. During the discussion of boyfriends, however, Mirna was surprised to learn that Jessica's boyfriend, Patrick O'Connor, was a bit of a bad boy. When the girls were friends at college, they were pretty conservative and had concentrated on their studies, but now Jessica was dating a young man with a completely different way of life. O'Connor was involved in drugs and alcohol, and his habits seemed to be rubbing off on Jessica.

Despite their solid friendship for many years, the two girls argued about Jessica's boyfriend. It was clear that Mirna disapproved of her dating a man that was such a bad influence on her and told her in no uncertain terms that she should get away from him. Mirna told her that this guy was messing up her future, and if she didn't change her path, it would change her life forever.

Jessica didn't take the advice well and told Mirna that she loved Patrick despite his faults and would stick with him. She became furious with Mirna to the point that Mirna was uncomfortable being alone with her. The rest of her Sydney trip became awkward, and Mirna ensured that there was always another friend with them whenever they went out.

Despite her initial objections, Jessica reluctantly took Mirna's advice and dumped her boyfriend. Still, Jessica secretly harbored deep resentment toward Mirna for suggesting that she leave the man she loved. Leaving him didn't stop her problems, though. They were only getting started.

After breaking up with Patrick, Jessica developed a drinking problem, and her attitude toward friends and co-workers began to change. Over the next two years, Jessica drank more and more until one night in August 2015 when, while driving drunk, she plowed her car over a curb, across a grassy area, and through the wall of a busy nursing home. Her vehicle landed within meters of the bedrooms of elderly residents. The fiasco landed her a DUI, a cracked rib, some time in jail, and an embarrassing video of her on the nightly news. Despite potentially killing residents of the nursing home, Jessica was angry rather than apologetic.

Throughout 2014 and 2015, Jessica attempted suicide five times. She was admitted to Royal Prince Alfred Hospital each time, and when she returned to work, she told her boss,

"Those bastards in the hospital didn't allow me to go home, and they treated me like a murderer. If I want to kill someone, I know exactly the right dose."

In October 2015, during one of her failed suicide attempts, Jessica tried to poison herself. Police found her unconscious, with a bottle of whiskey and three handwritten letters next to her bed. One letter blamed her ex-boyfriend, Patrick O'Connor, for her death. She addressed two other letters to her family and work friends, saying her goodbyes.

Jessica's anger and alcohol problems were affecting her work. She worked as a graphic designer at a firm called New South Wales Ambulance, but despite working there for less than a year, she developed deep-seated anger toward her boss, Kristie Carter. At one point, Jessica threatened Kristie because she wouldn't help Jessica find a place to stay after crashing her car into the nursing home, telling her, "You must die, and your mother must die." Kristie reported the threat to the local police.

Jessica regretted her breakup with Patrick and sent him countless text messages and voicemails. She threatened to hurt herself, him, and his friends if he didn't take her back. Patrick, however, wanted nothing to do with her. She was clearly unstable, and in December 2015, Australian police issued an urgent restraining order against her.

Back in Jakarta, Mirna was having the time of her life. Her picture-perfect life was that of a wealthy socialite: she had a well-paying job that she loved and was planning her dream wedding. But due to Jessica's continuing problems and their uncomfortable discussion, Mirna decided not to invite her to the wedding.

In her mind, Jessica already thought Mirna was to blame for her problems. Her downward spiral was all a result of Mirna's bad advice. As a result, her anger and resentment escalated when she wasn't invited to Mirna's wedding.

Mirna and Arief Soemarko had an island wedding in Bali in late 2015. The wedding ceremony was elaborate and straight out of a fairy tale. They had plans to honeymoon in Korea and wanted to start a family as soon as possible.

A few days after the wedding, Jessica continued her downward spiral and was fired from her graphic design job at New South Wales Ambulance. Now jobless, Jessica took some time to return to Jakarta and visit friends. She wanted to get together with Mirna, let her know that there were no hard feelings, and congratulate her on her wedding.

The two girls agreed to meet for coffee at 5:15 p.m. on January 6, 2016, but Mirna was apprehensive despite Jessica's assurance of good intentions. Mirna didn't want to visit with Jessica alone, so she asked their mutual friend, Hani, to accompany her. Hani had also attended Billy Blue College with them in Sydney.

Jessica arrived oddly early at Olivier, a trendy restaurant in the posh Grand Indonesia Shopping Mall in central Jakarta. Mirna thought it was unusual when Jessica texted her at 1 p.m., insisting she would pre-order the coffee for the three girls. Mirna assured her there was no need for that and that she would order when they arrived later that afternoon.

Jessica arrived at Olivier at 3:30 p.m., more than ninety minutes before Mirna and Hani were scheduled to arrive. She walked around the restaurant looking for the perfect table, then left the restaurant to do some shopping. She wanted to buy gifts for her friends, so she stopped at Bath & Body Works. Jessica purchased three small bottles of bath soap for the three of them and arrived back at Olivier at 4:14 p.m. with three large gift bags. The gift bags were unusually large for only having a single, small bottle of bath soap in them.

Security cameras showed Jessica walking around the entire restaurant, still looking for the perfect table and occasionally glancing directly at the cameras. After a few minutes of searching, she chose a half-circle booth on the side of the restaurant with large palm trees behind it. The palm trees behind the booth conveniently obscured the security camera behind them, leaving only a single security camera across the restaurant pointing directly at the table.

Jessica then placed the large gift bags on the table, waited a few moments, and then moved the bags toward the center of the table. Almost an hour before Mirna and Hani were due to arrive at the restaurant, Jessica ordered a Vietnamese iced coffee for Mirna and two additional coffee drinks for herself and Hani. When the drinks arrived at 4:24, Jessica was seen on the security camera doing something with the glasses, but the cameras didn't pick up the details because of the gift bags blocking the view.

The drinks then sat on the table for fifty-two minutes until Mirna and Hani arrived at 5:16. Within a few seconds of sitting down, Mirna took a big gulp of the Vietnamese iced coffee Jessica had ordered for her and immediately knew something was wrong. She began rapidly waving her arm in front of her mouth and told the girls something was wrong with the coffee. She pushed the glass away from her and continued frantically waving her hand. In less than sixty seconds, Mirna's head fell back against the top of the padded booth. Her eyes rolled back in her head, her body began to convulse violently, and she started foaming from her mouth.

Restaurant staff and other patrons of the restaurant started to gather around. Their first assumption was that Mirna had epilepsy and she was having a seizure. Hani, crying and panicking, called Mirna's husband. Jessica, however, showed no signs of stress at all.

Mirna was unresponsive, and emergency medical workers carried her out of the restaurant in a wheelchair, rushing her to the hospital. She died shortly afterward.

Jessica was the first person to make accusations. When people started gathering around at the restaurant, Jessica immediately said to the restaurant manager, Devi Siagian, "What did you put inside the drinks?!" Because of this accusation, Devi had the foresight to collect the three coffee glasses and save them in the back of the restaurant until the police arrived.

In the days after her death, it was assumed Mirna had died of an epileptic seizure, and Jessica and Hani were not questioned at the scene. However, three days after Mirna's death, when police analyzed the contents of the Vietnamese iced coffee, they realized she didn't die of an epileptic seizure at all. Mirna's drink had contained a lethal dose of cyanide; the case was now considered a homicide.

Mirna's family initially objected to an autopsy. Indonesia is a predominantly Muslim country, and it wasn't common for autopsies to be conducted as the procedure mutilates the body. However, the police assured the process would be brief. Finally Mirna's family agreed to an autopsy, and on January 10, the medical examiner found that there was bleeding in Mirna's stomach consistent with that of a corrosive substance. Traces of cyanide were found in her stomach but not in her other internal organs.

When police analyzed the security camera footage from the restaurant, they noticed Jessica awkwardly backing away from the scene while Mirna was convulsing. She made an odd movement with her hands, but exactly what she was doing was unclear. Speculation was that she was moving something from one hand to the other, while another theory was that she was scratching her finger because she had just stirred poison into Mirna's drink using that finger.

(A link to the security camera footage can be found in the online appendix at the end of this book.)

When the Grand Indonesian Police heard about the relationship problems between Jessica and Mirna, they turned to the authorities in Sydney to look into Jessica's background. While Australia had abolished the death penalty in the 1980s, it was still in effect in Indonesia and was carried out by firing squad. The Australian Federal Police only agreed to help investigate the case after assurances from the Indonesian government that prosecutors would not seek the death penalty.

The Australian Federal Police shared the confidential history of Jessica's troubles: her DUI charges, her multiple suicide attempts, her death threat to her former boss, and the restraining order her ex-boyfriend had issued against her. They also interviewed her former boss, Kristie Carter, for nine hours. Later, Kristie's testimony became vital evidence in the case against Jessica.

Within weeks, Indonesian Police officially charged Jessica with the murder of Mirna Salihin. Dressed in an orange prison jumpsuit and with a sign hanging around her neck with her name on it, police took Jessica back to the Olivier restaurant for a reenactment of the crime.

Indonesian news outlets and social media quickly became obsessed with the case, and Jessica was thrust into the public spotlight. Reporters and cameras followed Jessica's every step, and she seemed to strangely enjoy the attention. Television cameras showed Jessica smiling and waving as if she was unaware of the reason for all the attention.

Despite the agreement between the Australian Federal Police and the Grand Indonesian Police, prosecutors said the agreement not to seek the death penalty would be void if they convicted her on evidence the Jakarta police had gathered. The Indonesian police also argued that Jessica was not an Australian citizen but only a permanent resident. Eventually, the Indonesian police said they would leave it up to the judges for sentencing.

The case quickly became the most notorious case in Indonesian history. The media called Jessica "The Coffee Killer," and the public interest was overwhelming in both Indonesia and Australia. The case played out like a soap opera and was covered every night on the evening news. Everyone in Indonesia seemed to have an opinion of whether Jessica was innocent or guilty.

The broadcast media was criticized for spreading insensitive rumors that Jessica was having an affair with Mirna's husband. A coffee shop in Jakarta advertised non-toxic Vietnamese iced coffee with the slogan, "What doesn't kill you makes you stronger." The Olivier restaurant became a tourist attraction for those who wanted to see where the crime occurred.

The trial started on June 15, 2016, and Indonesian national television broadcast it live. Jessica's wealthy family hired Otto Hasibuan, a well-known celebrity defense lawyer. The defense team questioned the autopsy results, pointing out that they found no cyanide in any of Mirna's organs other than her stomach. They produced forensic and toxicology experts that testified there was no proof that cyanide caused her death.

Jessica took the stand in her own defense, explaining that Mirna was a friend with whom she could laugh, talk, and share secrets. She tried to play on the sympathy of the court,

"My family has been publicly shamed, and I have been treated like the scum of the earth since the case started."

Mirna's friends and family held press conferences to sway public opinion against Jessica.

The prosecution presented forty-six witnesses, including Mirna's father, husband, twin sister, and several employees from the restaurant. The prosecution presented the case with the motive of revenge. They argued that Jessica blamed Mirna for the breakup with her ex-boyfriend and the subsequent chain of events in Jessica's life.

The prosecution alleged that the security camera footage showed her looking around the restaurant to see if anyone was watching while she handled the coffee. They also argued that the murder was pre-meditated – that the use of poison illustrates pre-planning. They also used the interview with Jessica's former employer, where Jessica threatened her life, and the restraining order against her to show her anger consumed her.

Ultimately, the panel of three judges agreed with the prosecution. On October 27, 2016, after almost five months of trial, Jessica Wongso was found guilty of poisoning Mirna Salihin by putting cyanide in her coffee.

Jessica Wongso was sentenced to twenty years in prison. She and her team of lawyers submitted a lengthy appeal, but both the Jakarta High Court and the Supreme Court rejected it. Jessica Wongso had no option but to serve the remainder of her sentence.

CHAPTER 2
CAPTAIN CASH

I n the late 1990s, London had a thriving drug trade, and
Ken Avery was a top-level heroin dealer living the high
life. Avery was well-dressed, making money hand over
fist, and known for always having a briefcase full of cash
with him, which earned him the nickname "Captain Cash."
Avery had been smuggling drugs, selling fake passports, and
laundering money on a massive scale. In 1996, he was
involved in an elaborate plan to smuggle £40 million worth
of marijuana into the UK using a submarine.

Avery was known as a playboy that showered women he was
interested in with lavish gifts, once buying a woman a new
car when hers couldn't be repaired. When he met London
socialite Belinda Bruin, he was instantly smitten. Belinda was
the personal assistant of Bob Geldof's wife, Paula Yates, and
was also involved in the London drug scene. She had previously been arrested with the trunk of her car full of cocaine.

Avery tried hard to impress Belinda, offering to take her by
private helicopter to the Monaco Grand Prix, but she

declined most of his offers of affection. Finally, however, she accepted his gift of a £4,000 Cartier watch.

Avery ran a bonded warehouse in London which was a perfect cover for his smuggling business. On June 17, 1998, however, his extravagant lifestyle ended when he was caught with twenty-five kilos of heroin and led police on a high-speed pursuit.

Avery was facing over twenty years in prison, but prosecutors offered him a deal. They offered to reduce his sentence to eight years if he helped prosecute the higher-level drug dealers he worked with. Avery took the offer, and his testimony helped put away twelve criminals in a cocaine ring with a business estimated to be worth over £2 billion.

At his sentencing, the judge said,

"As a result of your co-operation, you will never again be trusted by your former colleagues, so you can't go back [to a life of crime], and the enmity of those people will make your future life precarious… those who turn against former associates should receive a very great reduction in their sentence."

During his incarceration, one of his cellmates said,

> "He knew there were contracts on his life, but he didn't seem to care. His attitude was, 'Come on, then, let's get it over with.' There was no way he was going to live quietly. Believe me, when he goes, He will go out with a bang."

Even though his sentence had been reduced to eight years, Avery served only three and was released in 2002. After his release, he had very few friends and no money. Thus, he legally changed his name from Ken Avery to Ken Regan and moved in with his father in a tiny one-bedroom bungalow.

In July 2002, Regan was looking for a way to create his next fortune when he came across a freight company based at Heathrow Airport called CIBA Freight, owned by a man named Amarjit "Neil" Chohan.

CIBA Freight was a very successful fruit importer. Though forty-five-year-old Neil Chohan was wealthy, he was a very modest man. Having saved over £2 million, he could easily afford a luxurious home, but he and his twenty-five-year-old wife Nancy, mother-in-law, and two baby boys lived in a tiny bungalow near the airport. Though he could afford a fancy car, Neil drove his eight-year-old Ford Escort to work daily. Neil and Nancy had recently started their family, with their oldest son just eighteen months old and the newborn just two months old.

His employees knew Neil as a very easygoing boss. Most of them considered him a friend and described him as happy-go-lucky. His relaxed demeanor came into play when Ken Regan came in to apply for a job. Although Regan was an ex-convict, Neil still gave him a chance. After all, Neil had spent a short time in prison for tax evasion. He believed every man deserved a second chance at life and offered Regan a job as a delivery driver.

Ken Regan was a hard worker and quickly gained the trust of Neil Chohan and the other employees. After working for CIBA for six months, Regan came to Neil with a proposal. He explained that he knew some investors in the Salisbury area, near Stonehenge, who were interested in buying CIBA Freight. They were prepared to offer him £3 million for his business. But the investors were fictional; his story was just a plan to take over CIBA Freight and use it for smuggling drugs again. Regan was determined to regain his drug empire at any cost.

Though Belinda Brewin hadn't contacted Regan during his three years in prison, he was still obsessed with the woman. She had since sold her home in Chelsea, London, and moved to a large country estate in Devon. Regan visited her and took notice of her sprawling ranch. He told her she should make some improvements: cut down some trees, build a nice secure wall with electric gates, and put in some drainage for the muddy roads that meandered through the property. She found it strange that he made all these suggestions for changes but thought nothing further of it.

In early February, Regan drove to see Belinda and told her he had some news. He was planning on taking over CIBA Freight and offered her £72,000 per year to manage it for him. He explained that she would only have to work two days a week and she agreed.

Neil initially wasn't interested in selling the company, but after speaking to his wife, Nancy, about the prospect, they agreed it might be a good idea. She wanted him to retire and the family to move to India so they could raise their children in better schools than the ones the UK had to offer. So, on February 13, 2003, Neil Chohan agreed to meet Regan's associates. That Thursday morning, Neil told his employees he was driving down near Stonehenge for a meeting. That was the last time they saw him.

The following Monday morning, the employees of CIBA Freight were called to an emergency meeting held by Ken Regan. He announced that Neil Chohan had agreed to sell the company, and Belinda Brewin was the new owner. Regan told the employees that Neil wished them well, but Nancy was in ill health; he had decided to retire and move back to India to raise his family.

Regan then showed them a bill of sale for the company, signed by Neil Chohan. The employees were shocked, but ultimately, it was a busy company; they needed to get back to business as usual.

The next day, as Belinda was driving to her new job at CIBA Freight, she was feeling sick and turned around to return home. As she was pulling onto her property, she encountered two men with an older model Jaguar and digging equipment. The men had a backhoe and were digging a large trench on one of the roads on her property. Furious, she stopped the car, confronted the men, and asked what they were doing. She hadn't ordered any work to be done. The men explained that Ken Regan had sent them to put in a drainage pipe and put gravel over the muddy road. Belinda was furious, but Regan eventually convinced her to let him install the drainage.

———

Twelve thousand miles away in New Zealand, Nancy Chohan's older brother, Onkar Verma, was getting worried. Although he hadn't seen his sister in nine years, the two were still extremely close and spoke on the phone daily.

On February 14, he received a frantic call from his sister. She was terrified. She had received a call from a worker at CIBA Freight that told her Neil had flown to Holland. Nancy knew that that couldn't be true because she knew he didn't have his passport with him. Then she received a voicemail message from her husband in English. The two usually spoke to each other in Punjabi, never English.

The next day, Onkar tried to call his sister and his mother, but there was no reply. All calls after that came to an abrupt halt.

Panicked, Onkar called CIBA Freight and spoke to a manager there named Mike Parr. Parr told him that Neil and his family had sold the company and moved back to India, but Onkar knew that couldn't be true. Nancy and Neil would never do that without telling him. He knew something was horribly wrong. Parr even faxed Onkar a power of attorney document signed by Neil, which only alarmed him more: Neil's signature was nothing more than a scribble.

On February 19, Onkar emailed Scotland Yard to explain his worries, and they referred him to the missing person unit.

> "I spoke to Nancy every day. There's never been a day when we did not speak. My sister rang me twice a day, my mum also, and every day, I would ring them once. All of a sudden, there're no calls, no call to say we're OK or we're going to India."

London police told him they stopped by and did a welfare check, but the house was empty. Police told him that the neighbors and friends confirmed that they had moved back to India. Onkar knew none of this could be true and on March 5, he booked a flight to London.

When he arrived, Onkar got the keys to the family home from Mr. Parr at Neil's office and went to the house.

When he arrived he found clothes still in the washing machine, cooked meals in the fridge, and the boy's feed bottles filled. It was clear they had left in a hurry and Onkar became even more worried.

Because Neil Chohan had been in jail for tax evasion in the past, Onkar believed that the police assumed he was in trouble again and was running from someone.

> "I believe they racially stereotyped him, obviously. The police kept saying he's done a runner because he was in trouble. I never believed the police story because I was very close to my family, and they would have told me about it."

Eventually, he convinced the police to transfer the case to the serious crimes group when he explained that his mother's most precious possession, her prayer book, was still in the house, and she went nowhere without it.

The first person detectives interviewed was the last to see Neil Chohan – Ken Regan. Regan told police that Chohan was a shady businessman and had gotten into financial trouble. He said that his only choice was to flee back to India.

After researching Neil Chohan's business dealings, investigators were skeptical of Regan's story and began investigating him instead. They immediately found his extensive criminal background, then looked into his and Neil's phone records.

Cell phone location tracking showed that Chohan left his home in Hounslow and drove toward Stonehenge on February 13. Regan lived nearby in Wilton, Salisbury, and police noticed that Regan's phone met with Chohan's near Stonehenge, then both phones traveled further south.

Knowing that Belinda was now managing CIBA and the two phones had traveled near her home, detectives called her to tell her that they were driving down to question her. Belinda agreed, but Regan was furious with her. He didn't want the police coming onto her property, so he told her to call them back and tell them she would meet them elsewhere.

Belinda didn't understand why he would want her to do that, but she didn't need to call them after all. Regan always had a plan.

Police suddenly received a lead on the whereabouts of Neil Chohan. That lead came from an associate of Regan, William Horncy. Horncy and Regan had sold stolen passports together years ago, and Regan had testified against him, landing him in prison. At the direction of Regan, Horncy called the detectives. He explained that he knew Neil Chohan was still in the UK because he and Regan had plans to meet him the following week in Newport, Wales. He claimed Chohan wanted to buy five stolen passports from him.

Rather than questioning Belinda, detectives decided to wait a few days and see if Chohan showed up to buy the passports. That meant they called Belinda and told her they wouldn't need to question her after all.

Regan had still been pressing Belinda to put in more drainage on her property, and she had eventually agreed to let him put in a ditch near the horse stables, so she wasn't surprised when the same two men she had seen before showed up again with a backhoe. She took her kids to town for the day while the men worked.

The following Monday, detectives watched Regan and Horncy standing near a bronze statue of a pig in Newport. That was to be the meeting point for the sale of the stolen passports. However, as police watched, Regan received a phone call. It seemed the meeting wasn't happening; detectives had a sinking feeling that Regan and Horncy had tricked them. The meeting had been pure fiction.

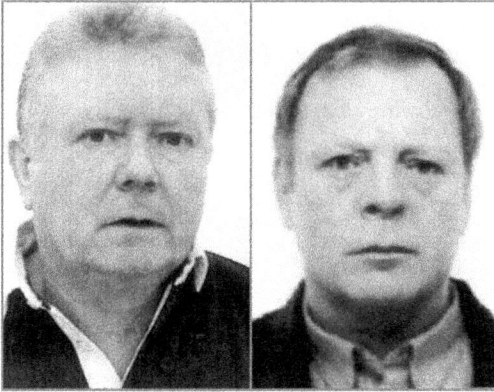

Kenneth Regan & William Horncy

On April 22, detectives again wanted to interview Belinda Brewin and drove to her home. During the interview, they asked if she had noticed anything odd about Regan's behavior in the past few days, and she mentioned that she had. When she told Regan the police wanted to interview her, he said,

"If they ask you what I was doing on your land, just tell them I was helping you with your water system."

Detectives asked what he really did on her land, and she told them he had dug a drainage ditch. They knew what that meant and immediately assembled a team to dig up Belinda's property.

———

Later that same afternoon, a father and son were spending the evening on a kayak trip off the coast of Bournemouth when they noticed something floating in the ocean. As they got closer, they could tell it was a body. As evening fell, the boy paddled into shore and alerted the police, while the father waited for three hours on the dark ocean with the bloated body, until police arrived.

The body had suffered severe blunt trauma to the back of the head. Packing tape was still wrapped tightly around the head and jaw. One week after they found it, investigators positively identified the body as that of Neil Chohan. The cause of death was both blunt force trauma and suffocation. Police still had no idea where the rest of the family was, but it was becoming increasingly clear that they were dead as well.

The evidence from the body suggested that Neil Chohan had been buried in the ground, then exhumed at a later date and transported to a boat, where he was dumped into the water.

Detectives brought in forensic archeologists and pathologists to dig through the area of the drainage ditch on Belinda Brewin's property. They had found nothing after five days of painstakingly sifting through the dirt, but the site was huge, so the forensic team continued searching. Eventually, they recovered jewelry that belonged to Nancy Chohan, baby clothes, and evidence of a large bonfire. Unfortunately there were still no bodies, but detectives assumed that they had buried the entire family there at one time.

Further analysis of phone location records revealed a chain of events on the day Chohan went missing. It showed that when Chohan met Regan at Stonehenge, two additional phones were traveling the same route. The phones belonged to William Horncy and another career criminal, Peter Rees.

By this time, all three of the suspects were on the run. Ken Regan and William Horncy had fled into mainland Europe, while Peter Rees was alone and in hiding in the United Kingdom.

Peter Rees had checked into a boarding house and had a guilty conscience. He confessed to a woman at the boarding house that the police wanted him for murder, but he claimed that he didn't do it. He told her that Regan had killed all five of the Chohan family. The woman called the police, and Rees spent three days running but was arrested in a pub in Coleford. When police interrogated Rees, he refused to say anything about the Chohan family or his partners.

One month after Rees' arrest, a second body was found by fishermen floating off the coast of the Isle of Wight. Autopsy results confirmed it was the body of Nancy Chohan.

After two more months on the run in Spain, Regan fled to Belgium, where he was tracked down by police and returned to the United Kingdom. Horncy was still in hiding, but after another month, he became tired of running, returned to the UK, and turned himself in. Just one week later, the body of Nancy's mother, Charanjit Kaur, washed up on the shores of the Isle of Wight.

Detectives collected more evidence in preparation for the trial. Vital details came from the movements of the cell phones, as well as evidence provided by Horncy's own son. A final clue came from Neil Chohan himself.

By tracing the movement of their cell phones, investigators discovered that all four phones traveled from Stonehenge to Wilton in Salisbury. The phones arrived at a small bungalow at the address 3 Forge Close. It was the small home that Ken Regan shared with his father. The men had held Neil Chohan captive there for the next three days.

William Horncy's son willingly gave the police a Lexmark color printer and a gray suitcase. Upon examining the suitcase, the police found ten sheets of blank computer paper with Neil Chohan's signature on them. Regan threatened Chohan and made him sign the blank sheets of paper while he was being held captive. Regan planned to use the signatures to print documents for the takeover of CIBA Freight and to forge additional documents in the future.

The movement of the phones also showed that on February 15, Regan and Horncy then traveled back to London to the Chohan's home. Prosecutors believed Nancy Chohan, her baby sons Ravinder and Devinder, and her mother, Charanjit Kaur, were all murdered that day. Regan and Horncy then rented a van and transported the bodies south to Belinda Brewin's property, where they buried them in the drainage ditch.

The most vital piece of evidence came from Neil Chohan himself. While he was held captive at 3 Forge Close, Neil Chohan managed to find a letter in the house where he was being held. He carefully folded and tucked the letter into his right sock. Though it was damaged from being buried and then dumped in the ocean, the letter remained intact in his sock.

The letter was from Cheltenham & Gloucester Building Society addressed to:

Mr. KR Regan & Mr. RF Avery,

3 Forge Close,

South Newton, Salisbury Wiltshire SP2 OQG.

The date on the letter was February 22, 2003, the day before he was abducted.

Neil Chohan knew he would be murdered, and although he faced certain death, he wanted to leave a clue as to who killed him.

The trial began on November 8, 2004, and lasted nine months. It was the longest criminal trial in UK history and cost taxpayers over £10 million. Prosecutors presented almost 4,500 exhibits of evidence. All three suspects pleaded not guilty and claimed they were falsely imprisoned.

Peter Rees was convicted of Neal Chohan's murder but cleared of the other four murders and received twenty-three years in prison. Horncy and Regan were both sentenced to five consecutive life sentences without the possibility of parole.

The bodies of eighteen-month-old Devinder and eight-week-old Ravinder were never recovered.

Eleven years later, in 2016, police linked both Regan and Horncy to the death of Michael Schallamach from Southampton. When Schallamach went missing in 1992, police and his family were told that he had run off to Europe and Nigeria with an unknown woman. The family received a handwritten letter from someone, allegedly calling herself Helen, saying they had been living together in Europe. However, the last person to ever see Michael Schallamach was Kenneth Regan.

CHAPTER 3

THE OXFORD MURDER

R achel McLean had traveled back home to Blackpool, UK, to stay with her parents during the summer break of 1990. The eighteen-year-old had just finished her first year at St. Hilda's College in Oxford, UK, where she had a hectic schedule with school and social groups. She was an active environmentalist and a vegetarian, but her friends also knew her to be a party girl that loved heavy metal. During term breaks, she worked part-time jobs and donated her time to local charities.

Late that summer, Rachel and her friends were drinking at the Adam & Eve club when she met John Tanner, a charming bartender with long brown hair.

John was from Nottingham, a few hours away, and was working a summer job in Blackpool. He was good-looking, sociable, outgoing, and funny. John was born in the United Kingdom but immigrated to New Zealand at an early age. After growing up in New Zealand, he returned to the UK to attend university in Nottingham and live with his aunt.

Rachel and John flirted that night and by the end of the evening, she had invited him to her upcoming nineteenth birthday party. John gladly accepted. When he showed up for her birthday party, John and Rachel instantly hit it off. They slept together that night, and the relationship developed from there.

At the end of the summer, Rachel returned to Oxford, John to Nottingham. Oxford was over two hours away from Nottingham, so they could only see each other during occasional long weekends or holidays. He called her several times a week and wrote her a steady stream of long love letters.

That December, she invited him to spend Christmas with her family. She brought him to Blackpool to meet her parents and gave him a paisley tie as a Christmas present.

Rachel McLean and John Tanner

Over the months, John grew increasingly infatuated with Rachel, but the distance frustrated him. He became agitated when he called the flat she shared with four other students to find she wasn't home.

But Rachel was a busy girl who was involved with her studies and many social groups. She didn't have time to wait by the phone for him to call. Each time he called, his jealousy stewed. He worried that she was seeing other men. Her roommates noticed that they regularly argued over the phone about his jealousy issues.

Although she wouldn't tell him directly, Rachel felt annoyed by his jealousy and thought he was overly possessive. So on February 11, she mailed him a Valentine's Day card in which she wrote:

"To my one and only John. The one who was with me through the most wondrous moments of my life."

But on the same day, she wrote her true feelings privately in her diary:

"What a joke. I just wrote John's Valentine's card. Full of sweet, pure words. Words that I shoveled out of some fountain inside me. A fountain that dried and cracked. Somehow, I don't think you would have appreciated sweet nothings along the lines of 'you sick childish bastard.'"

Unaware of her true feelings, he professed his love to Rachel that Valentine's day and asked her to marry him. To his disappointment, she turned him down.

In April, Rachel spent the Easter break with her parents in Blackpool. The Saturday after Easter, Rachel's mother drove her back to Oxford. After dropping her off, her mother returned to Blackpool around 4 p.m.; John arrived at 7:30 to spend the rest of the weekend with her.

That Sunday was a lazy day at home for the couple. Rachel's roommates hadn't returned from the holidays yet, so Rachel and John had the flat all to themselves. Rachel had term exams the following week, so she studied in the front room while John watched football. John was an avid Nottingham fan, and they were playing West Ham in the FA Cup semi-finals.

The following evening, John took the 6:55 train back to Nottingham from the Oxford train station.

Later that week, when her roommates returned home, Rachel wasn't there. Her bedroom windows were open, but nothing seemed to be out of place. They thought it was odd, but they knew Rachel was busy with school, so they weren't concerned. John tried to call on Wednesday but got no answer, then tried the following day and, as usual again, left a message with her roommates. The next day, a letter from John arrived in the mailbox. He had mailed it as soon as he returned to Nottingham.

"My dearest, lovely Rachel, thank you for such a lovely week-end. Please excuse the handwriting as I am now sadly wending my way away from your smiling face.

Fancy seeing that friend of yours at the station. At least you didn't have to get a bus home. It was nice of him to give you a lift. But I hate him because he has longer hair than me. Ha ha! It's nice to know you will not be alone for the next few days. I worry for you in that house on your own."

It wasn't until four days later, on April 19, when Rachel didn't show up for an appointment with her tutor, that her roommates knew something was wrong. Rachel never would have missed that appointment. Her tutor reported her missing.

Police initially didn't take the missing person report with much urgency. They received dozens of missing person reports every month in the busy college town.

Investigators began searching for Rachel at the flat she shared with four other students: Victoria Clare, Margaret Smith, Sarah Heaume, and Jo Formby. During the questioning, her roommates showed police the letter John had mailed to Rachel from Nottingham. The letter's contents let them know that John was the last person to have contact with her – except for an unknown man at the Oxford train station.

Nothing seemed out of place during the first inspection of the house. There were no obvious signs of foul play and nothing was out of place. Initial examinations of the floorboards showed no signs of tampering, but when police later found Rachel's diary, they realized that John's letter didn't quite add up. From what Rachel had written in her diary, they could clearly see that John was very possessive of her. In his letter, he wrote of the "long-haired stranger" who gave her a ride back home, but that wasn't John's style. He wouldn't have been tolerant of another man taking her home. From her diary, investigators knew that this mysterious man would have set off John's jealousy. That never would have sat well with John.

A second letter from John arrived at Rachel's flat. It was short and sharp. He wrote,

> "I have tried calling you all week, but I guess you are working. A call would be appreciated."

The following Monday, April 22, police spoke to John Tanner in the first of many interviews. He expressed his concern for Rachel's whereabouts and told detectives that Rachel had woken up earlier than him the previous Monday to study while he slept in until around noon. He then showered and got ready to take the train back to Nottingham. He said they made love in the afternoon and took the bus to the Oxford train station around 4:15 p.m.

John claimed that while they were at Oxford Station waiting for his 6:55 p.m. train, they ran into a friend of Rachel's in the cafe, where the three of them sat and had coffee. He described the man as having long hair, ripped jeans, and a black leather jacket. The description was essentially the same as a description of himself. John explained that he didn't remember the man's name as he didn't think it was important at the time. However, he told the police that the mystery man had offered to take Rachel back to her house, so she wouldn't have to take the bus home.

John said that he and Rachel embraced and kissed on the platform before his train arrived, then he boarded the train back to Nottingham. But detectives didn't buy his story, and he quickly became the prime suspect.

That same day, the Oxford Police went public with the news of Rachel's disappearance. Detective John Bound told reporters,

"Although we could not admit it publicly, it seemed from the outset that some harm had befallen her. There was no reason for her to run away. She was a happy girl with a good background, loving parents, and a bright future."

Police assigned two police officers who befriended John Tanner. They made him believe they were updating him on the search for Rachel, but they were actually watching every move he made. They watched his reactions to the news of the investigation, his body language, and generally all of his movements from day to day.

The search of the neighboring area was extensive. Police went door to door in her neighborhood, asking neighbors if they had seen Rachel or noticed anything suspicious. Officers used sniffer dogs to comb through the nearby scrubland, and divers were sent to drag the nearby River Cherwell. Investigators searched Rachel's house once again, but again, they found nothing.

Nine days after Rachel's disappearance, her parents, Joan and Malcolm McLean, held a press conference in hopes it might help find their daughter. As with many mysteries like this, many calls came to the police with clues, but very few were of any help.

Police asked John to help them put together a sketch of the mystery man from the train station. However, when the drawing was released to the public, no one came forward with any information.

Rachel had been missing for two weeks, and detectives assumed the worst. They believed she was dead and had started searching sewers and cesspits around the Oxford area. Again, their efforts were futile.

Detectives still believed that John Tanner had killed her, but they needed concrete evidence. Surprisingly, Tanner agreed to participate in a press conference and a reconstruction of their last moments together at the Oxford train station. Tanner, however, saw it as an opportunity to portray himself as cooperative and willing to help with the investigation.

Detectives wanted to recruit the help of the media and asked a local television station to present specific questions to him during the press conference to see how he would react. During the press conference, reporters mentioned that his description of the mystery man was much like that of himself. He replied,

"I had nothing to do with her disappearance. I know what people are saying."

As instructed by the police, they asked him directly if he believed she was still alive. His response was,

"I did not kill her. I don't know what happened to her. In my heart of hearts, I know she is still alive."

However, he spoke in the video with a slight smirk on his face. Naturally, that did not sit well with the public or the police.

Finally, when reporters asked if he had a message for anyone that may be holding Rachel against her will, he said,

"I would appeal to them to come forward and tell us, just out of sheer consideration for her mother and father and myself."

During the reconstruction, Tanner and a police officer who played Rachel's role stood on the platform at the train station arm in arm. An actor dressed to match his description of the mystery man met them at the cafe in the station, where they sat at a table and had coffee. Over the next several days, the local television channels repeatedly aired the reconstruction.

When John Tanner took part in reconstructing their last moments together, he thought no one would remember a random couple at a train station two weeks prior, but he was wrong. Two witnesses distinctly remembered John Tanner on April 15 at the Oxford train station. But they placed him alone, not with a girl or another man. An Oxford resident named Jane Wynn-Jones told police she had sat next to him at the station. She described,

"He was agitated and seemed to be shuffling a lot and going in and out of a bag, which was on the floor next to him. He brought out a pad with thin paper and lines on it. He was writing in black ink."

Investigators now believed that this was when Tanner penned the letter to Rachel which he later mailed from Nottingham.

Bit by bit, other parts of John's story started to fall apart. John claimed that he and Rachel had boarded a city bus at 4:15 p.m. that day, but Oxford busses electronically tracked how many people boarded and paid at each stop. On the day and time of that stop, only one person had boarded the bus: John Tanner.

Detectives suspected that Rachel McLean's body was still in her house somewhere. However, it wasn't until they contacted the Oxford Council to get detailed layouts of the home on Argyle Street that they realized the houses on that street were underpinned, meaning there were small cavities of air space beneath the floorboards.

On Thursday, May 2, nineteen days after Rachel was last seen, detectives returned to the house again for a more thorough examination. When they crawled into the cupboards beneath the stairwell and pulled up the floorboards, they found the body of Rachel McLean. Her body had been crammed into a small space only eight inches high. The cold outdoor temperatures at that time of year had slowed the body's decomposition, and the ventilation of the house underpinning allowed any odors to go undetected.

Within an hour of finding the body, John Tanner was arrested in a pub in Nottingham. Initially, Tanner refused to answer any questions posed by the police, but the following day, he broke down and admitted that he'd killed his girlfriend. Tanner explained that on that Sunday evening, after watching the football game, he again asked her for her hand in marriage, but again, she turned him down. Finally, as he begged her, she became aggravated with him and told him she didn't want to be engaged. He wrote in his confession,

> "I was offended. I must have snapped. I flew at her in a rage and proceeded to put my hands around her neck. I think I must have lost control because I have only a vague recollection of the time that elapsed afterwards. I am bewildered why I have done such a terrible thing to a person I love dearly."

Tanner explained that they argued, and during the screaming, she admitted that she had been sleeping with other people. Tanner then called her a "tart." Rachel raised her hand as if she was going to slap him, but instead, he lost control. Tanner recalled lunging at her and moving his hands toward her neck. Medical examiners confirmed evidence of a ligature being used on her neck, but Tanner claimed that, if that happened, he had blacked it out. He said his only other recollection was sitting on the bed with her body on the floor. Police believe he used the paisley tie she gave him for Christmas to strangle her.

Tanner picked up Rachel's dead body and laid her on the bed, then slept on the floor next to her bed.

The following day, he pulled up the floorboards under the stairs and wedged her body into a tiny eight-inch gap beneath the floorboards. He then took a bus to the Oxford train station and caught the 6:55 p.m. train back to Nottingham.

As he waited at the station for the train, he wrote a letter to Rachel to make it appear that he believed her to still be alive and placed suspicion on the mystery man. He mailed the letter when he arrived home in Nottingham. In the days following, he called her home twice and sent a second letter in feeble attempts to solidify his alibi.

Seven months later, in December 1991, John Tanner pleaded not guilty despite his confession. He admitted to killing her, but he claimed it was not murder. Tanner knew that he would be handed a life sentence if he admitted to the murder and would serve about fifteen years. However, if he was convicted of manslaughter on the grounds of diminished responsibility, he would only get about eight years in prison and could be out in four or five. It was an easy choice.

Tanner played the role of the poor boyfriend in court. He tried to convince the jury that he was a loving, caring boyfriend that only wanted to marry his one true love, not the possessive control freak the prosecution made him out to be. He claimed that Rachel provoked him to lose his self-control. He claimed Rachel often teased him because he was unable to perform sexually due to pain from a groin injury.

Ultimately, his pleas didn't help him. After four hours of deliberation, the jury returned with a 10-2 majority guilty verdict.

At his sentencing, Judge Kennedy told Tanner,

"I entirely accept that she was precious to you, but this was a savage attack. And your conduct afterwards, up until the time when her body was found, did nothing to ameliorate the gravity of the offense."

Despite it all, Rachel's mother said that she forgave Tanner,

"I think we feel the way we have always felt - that this is a tragedy for him in his life as well. Yes, I think we can forgive

him because otherwise, it eats into your life and the lives of
others around you. If you start on the path of forgiveness,
you can start to build a new life, and all the people around
you can build new lives."

Twenty-two-year-old John Tanner was sentenced to life in
prison, but that's not the end of the story. While in prison, he
formed an odd relationship with a 26-year-old woman
named Siobahn Howes, who bore a striking resemblance to
Rachel McLean. Siobhan visited Tanner at Gartree Prison
while studying criminology at Loughborough University.

Siobahn saw Tanner as a victim of a tragic chain of circumstances and a crime of passion. During his time in prison,
Tanner referred to Siobahn as his girlfriend, and she looked
into the possibility of Tanner finishing his prison sentence in
New Zealand.

She eventually moved to New Zealand and taught at
Wanganui Collegiate School, the same school Tanner had
attended years earlier.

After serving only a little more than eleven years of his life
sentence, Tanner was released in 2003 and returned to New
Zealand. It is unknown whether Tanner got together with
Siobahn Howes upon his return to New Zealand, but he was
back in the news again in 2018.

Over a period of six months in 2017, Tanner abused his girlfriend repeatedly and threatened to kill her.

At forty-nine years old, Tanner was sentenced to two years
and nine months for punching her with a closed fist and
choking his girlfriend during an argument in New Zealand.

During his sentencing, Judge Crayton said,

"Between 1 March 2017 and 27 September 2017, whilst there was an argument, she told you she was leaving you. You, in response, told her that she was not, that you would kill her.

She did not take the threat seriously.

You then jumped on top of her and put both hands across her neck, restricting her breathing. As a consequence, she suffered soreness to her throat area.

You held her down, straddling her. You were yelling at her about her ex-partner. You used your hands to deliver blows, and slaps to her face and head a number of times.

You then punched her twice around the head with a closed fist. At that point, she had suffered a graze and bruising to the left side of her forehead.

She became worried and sat against the headboard on the bed with her knees up. You walked over and pulled her pants down and underwear off, saying you wanted sex.

It was said in a blunt and aggressive manner. You then demanded that she remove her SIM card from her phone, and as she attempted to get away from you, you grabbed her by the shirt, pulling her forward, and punching her several times in the head.

The victim fell onto the floor and attempted to shield her face from the blows. You punched the victim around the head and face several more times.

Mr. Tanner, it is, of course, and never has been acceptable for violence within a family context. You have one signifi-cant aggravating factor; it is your previous conviction for murder.

Your uttering of your intent to have sex with her is a disturbing element. That you ripped her clothing off can only be seen in this context as an act of violent domination and control over your victim.

On charge three, injuring with intent to injure, the sentence is one of two years, nine months. On charge one and charge two, there will be one year's imprisonment, concurrent on each."

CHAPTER 4
GOD CHOSE US

T he late spring of 1985 was hot in Lexington County, South Carolina, and seventeen-year-old Sharon "Shari" Faye Smith spent the day with her boyfriend, Richard, and a few other friends swimming at nearby Lake Murray.

It was May 31, the Friday before high school graduation, and they were all excited about the graduation ceremony that Sunday. Shari loved to sing and was scheduled to sing the national anthem at their graduation. Immediately afterward, she and her friends had tickets to go on a cruise to the Bahamas.

After leaving the lake, Richard followed behind Shari's car and watched as she turned off the main highway toward her home on Platt Springs Road. The Smiths' home sat back 750 feet from the lonely rural road, with a long driveway leading up to the house. When her little light-blue Chevy Chevette pulled into the driveway at 3:38 that afternoon, her father, Robert, was working in his home office. From his window at the front of the house, he watched as Shari stopped to get the mail from the mailbox on the side of the road, just as she always did before she finished the drive up to the house.

Shari's father continued his work, expecting her to come in the door any minute. But when ten minutes passed and she hadn't come in, he peered out the window again. There at the end of the driveway, he saw the car. The driver's side door was still open but there was no sign of Shari.

Robert got in his own car and drove down the long driveway to see if she needed help. Or maybe she had stopped to talk to someone. But when he got to the end of the driveway, the car was still running with the door still open. Shari was gone.

Bare footprints in the soft dirt led to the mailbox and pieces of mail lay on the ground, but the footprints didn't lead back to the car. Instead, they disappeared near the road. Inside the car, Mr. Smith found her towel, black jelly shoes, and purse, with her medication still sitting on the passenger seat.

Shari Smith suffered from diabetes insipidus, also known as water diabetes. This rare form of diabetes caused her to have an insatiable thirst and a need to constantly drink excessive amounts of water. Unfortunately, this also meant that she had to urinate very frequently. Initially, he thought she might have run across the street into the woods to urinate, but after calling out her name, he got no reply. Knowing that Shari would never go very far without her medication, he panicked. He raced back to the house and immediately called the Lexington County Sheriff.

As with any missing teenager report, police initially assumed Shari had run away from home. However, when Robert explained that her car was left running and that her condition could be fatal if she went without her medication, they sprang into action and put together a search team.

Within hours, Sheriff James Metts, a graduate of the FBI's National Academy, put together the largest organized manhunt in South Carolina history. The Emergency Preparedness Division set up a mobile command center in front of the Smiths' home. They parked a large trailer on their property equipped with radios and telephones and manned the trailer twenty-four hours a day rather than traveling to the local Sheriff's office.

Shari's boyfriend, Richard, and other friends and family were quickly eliminated as suspects. Word spread rapidly through the tight-knit community and the Smith family were overwhelmed with food contributions from neighbors. Anything they could do to help. But Shari's mother, Hilda couldn't eat. She was terrified. She paced the living room floor waiting for word that someone had found her missing daughter.

By Saturday evening, police believed that Shari had been abducted, possibly by a kidnapper hoping to receive a ransom for her safe return. Shari's parents waited by the phone all day that Saturday, but the only call was a cruel prank.

Sunday, the day that Shari was due to sing at her graduation, came and went. The only clue that police had received was from two young men who had driven down Platt Springs Road and recalled seeing Shari at the mailbox. They said they briefly saw a reddish-purple car coming toward them driven by a man in his thirties. They believed the vehicle was possibly a 1982-84 Oldsmobile Cutlass.

Early Monday morning at 2:20 a.m., the phone finally rang. The male caller used an electronic voice distortion device to hide his identity. The man demanded to speak to Shari's mother, Hilda. He wanted to prove that the call was not a hoax and described in detail the clothes that Shari was wearing that Friday. He perfectly described the yellow and black bathing suit she wore beneath her clothes that day. He then told Hilda she would receive a letter in the mail later that day. He informed her that the top of the letter would be dated 6/1/85, and the time would read 3:10 a.m. He then explained that the actual time the letter was written was 3:12, but he decided to round it off. He ended the call by telling her,

"They are looking in the wrong place. Tell Sheriff Metts to get on TV at 7:00 a.m. on Channel 10 and call off the search."

The call was traced to a pay phone twelve miles away from the Smiths' home, but when police arrived, the caller was nowhere to be found. The phone was checked for fingerprint evidence; he had wiped the phone clean, and nobody recalled seeing anyone using the pay phone.

Though the call was not recorded, Mrs. Smith took notes. The caller reassured her that Shari was fine. He told her she ate a little, drank lots of water, and watched TV, but there was no mention of a ransom.

Not wanting to waste precious time for the mail to be delivered, Sheriff Metts called the Lexington County Postmaster and opened the Post Office in the middle of the night so they could sort through the coming day's mail. By 7 a.m., they found a letter addressed to the Smith family. It was a white legal size envelope with a small piece of blue-lined paper pasted on the outside bearing the Smiths' address and no return address.

Inside the envelope were two sheets of lined yellow legal paper. Both pages were handwritten in Shari's handwriting. The first page was titled at the top, "Last Will & Testament."

The text was disheartening,

"6/1/85, 3:10 a.m.

I Love Ya'll

I love you, Mommy, Daddy, Robert, Dawn & Richard, and everyone else and all the other friends and relatives. I'll be with my father now, so please, don't worry! Just remember my witty personality & great special times we all shared together. Please don't ever let this ruin your lives just keep living one day at a time for Jesus. Some good will come out of this. My thoughts will always be with you & in you! (Casket closed). I love you all so damn much. Sorry dad, I had to cuss for once! Jesus forgave me. Richard sweetie - I really did & always will love you & treasure our special moments. I ask one thing though. Accept Jesus as your personal savior. My family has been the greatest influence of my life. Sorry about the cruise money. Some day go in my place.

I am sorry if I ever disappointed you in any way. I only wanted to make you proud of me because I have always been proud of my family. Mom, Dad, Robert & Dawn there's so much I want to say that I should have said before now I love you! I know y'all love me and will miss me very much, but if ya'll stick together like we always did - y'all can do it!

Please do not become hard or upset. Everything works out for the good of those that love the Lord.

I Love Y'all

W/All My Heart

Sharon (Shari) Smith

P.S. Nana - I love you so much. I kind of always felt like your favorite. You were mine! I Love you A lot."

6/1/85   3:10 AM   I Love ya!!

Last Will & Testament

G
O
D

i
S

L
O
V
E

Shorthand
♡

I love you mann, dad,
adret, Dawn, + Richard and
everyone else and all other
friends and relatives. I'll be
with my father now, so
please, please don't worry!
Just remember me with
personality & great special times
we all shared together. Please
don't even let this ruin your
lives, just keep living one day
at a time for Jesus. Some good
will come out of this. My
thoughts will always be with &
in you. (casket closed) I love you
all so damn much. Sorry dad,
I had to cuss for once! Jesus,
forgave me! Richard sweetie - I
really did & always will love
you & treasure our special
moments. I ask one thing that,
accept Jesus as your personal
savior. ☺ ③ My family has been
the greatest influence of my life.
Sorry about the cruise & more! Some
day please go in my place. ☺

Shari Smith Last Will & Testament Pg1

I am sorry if I ever disappointed you in any way. I only wanted to make you proud of me. Because I have always been proud of my family. Mom, dad, Robert & David I love you so much I want to say that I should have said before now! I ❤ you!

I know y'all love me and will miss me very much but if y'all stick together like we always did - y'all can do it!

Please do not become hard or upset. Everything works out for the good for those that love the Lord. ☺

I love y'all   All My Love Always -
W/ All My HEART ❤ Sharon (Shari) Smith

P.S. Nana - I love you so much. I kind of always felt like your favorite. You were mine.
I love you alot

Shari Smith Last Will & Testament Pg2

Near the top of the first page, in the left sidebar, she wrote, "God is Love" vertically and "ShaRichard" with a heart.

The letter was sent to the forensic document examiners who searched for clues. Many fingerprints were found on the pages, but they all belonged to Shari. However, the most important clue came from the latent indentations on the pages. The paper had come from a yellow-lined legal pad, and it was clear that the pad had been used in the past, as indentations from previous notes were visible.

Document examiners used an electrostatic detection apparatus (EDSA) to try and read the latent indentations. The device increased the humidity of the paper, which amplified the electrical conductivity. The paper was then placed on top of a brass plate, and a magnetic field was activated. It was then brushed with a black powder, showing the paper's prior indentations.

The process brought out latent indentations of what seemed to be partial phone numbers and a shopping list. The only readable words were "beef sticks," "Mother," "Bob," and the letters "J" and "S."

———

Later that Monday at 3:08 p.m., the phone rang at the Smith home. This time, investigators were ready to record the call. Shari's twenty-one-year-old sister Dawn answered the phone. Again, the voice was electronically distorted:

Dawn: "Hello."

Kidnapper: "Mrs. Smith."

Dawn: "No, this is Dawn."

Kidnapper: "I need to speak to your mother."

Dawn: "Could I ask who is calling?"

Kidnapper: "No."

Dawn: "Ok, hold on just a second, please."

———

Hilda: "Hello."

Kidnapper: "Have you received the mail today?"

Hilda: "Yes, I have."

Kidnapper: "Do you believe me now?"

Hilda: "Well, I'm not really sure I believe you because I haven't had any word from Shari, and I need to know that Shari is well."

Kidnapper: "You'll know in two or three days."

Hilda: "Why two or three days?"

Kidnapper: "Call the search off."

Hilda: "Tell me if she is well because of her disease. Are you taking care of her?"

———

The caller hung up. Investigators traced the call to a pay phone seven miles away at the Lexington Town Square Shopping Center, but the caller was gone by the time they got there, and there were no fingerprints on the telephone.

The search was expanded to include the entire state of South Carolina, the FBI was called in, and an alert went out to all law enforcement agencies nationwide.

That Monday, the Smith family decided to talk to television reporters. They hoped that the kidnapper would see how much suffering he had caused in the family and release Shari. During the press coverage, her father pleaded,

"Whoever has our daughter, Shari, we want her back. We miss her. We love her. Please send her back home. She belongs here with us."

A neighbor, Mrs. Terry Butler, saw the broadcast and contacted the police. She had driven in front of the Smiths' home that Friday and recalled seeing Shari pulling into the driveway. After passing the Smiths' house, she was met head-on by a car coming toward her in her lane. She blew her horn at the car, and the man quickly swerved back into his lane. She said the man was leaning over in the middle of the car and not paying attention to the road. She then watched in her rearview mirror and saw the car pull over near the Smiths' mailbox. Mrs. Butler described the driver as a white male who was slightly balding. Her description seemed to match what the two men had seen, and she helped police produce a sketch of the subject.

———

That evening at 8:07 p.m., the phone rang at the Smith house again. It was the same electronically distorted male voice. Dawn answered,

Dawn: "Hello."

Kidnapper: "Dawn, did you come down from Charlotte?"

Dawn: "Yes, I did; who's calling, please?"

Kidnapper: "I need to speak with your mother."

Dawn: "Ok, she's coming."

Kidnapper: "Tell her to hurry."

Dawn: "She's hurrying. Tell Shari I love her."

Kidnapper: "Did y'all receive her letter today?"

Dawn: "Yes, we did. Here's mother."

————

Hilda: "This is Hilda."

Kidnapper: "Did you receive Shari Rae's [sic] letter?"

Hilda: "Pardon? I can't hear you. It's not very clear. Speak louder."

Kidnapper: "Did you receive the letter today?"

Hilda: "Uh, yes, I did."

Kidnapper: "Tell me one thing it said. Hurry."

Hilda: "ShaRichard."

Kidnapper: "Do what?"

Hilda: "There was a little heart on the side, ShaRichard written on the side."

Kidnapper: "How many pages?"

Hilda: "Two pages."

Kidnapper: "Ok, and it was a yellow legal pad?"

Hilda: "Yes."

Kidnapper: "And on one side of the front page, it said, 'Jesus is love?'"

Hilda: "No, God is love."

Kidnapper: "Well, God is love."

Hilda: "Right."

Kidnapper: "Ok, so you know now this is not a hoax call?"

Hilda: "Yes, I know that."

Kidnapper: "I'm trying to do everything possible to answer some of your prayers, so please, in the name of God, work with us here."

Hilda: "Can you answer me one question, please? You... you are very kind... and, and you seem to be a compassionate person and... and I think you know how I feel being Shari's mother and how much I love her. Can you tell me? Is she all right physically without her medication?"

Kidnapper: "Shari is drinking a little over two gallons of water per hour and using the bathroom right afterward. I've got to hurry now. Ok, now, this has gone too far. Please forgive me. Have an ambulance ready at any time at your house. And on Shari's request, she requests that only immediate family come and Sheriff Metts and the ambulance attendants. She don't want to make a circus out of this."

Hilda: "Right. Ok."

Kidnapper: "And where she said 'casket closed' in parentheses... if anything happens to me, she said her... one of her requests she did not put in there was to put her hands on her stomach... cross her hands like she was praying in the casket."

Hilda: "We don't want any harm to you. I… I promise. We just want Shari well and all right, ok?"

Kidnapper: "Ok, listen. Listen real carefully. I've got to hurry. I know these calls are being traced, correct? Ok, now listen."

Hilda: "Uh, is Shari with you, or can you tell me that?"

Kidnapper: "I will not say. Ok, now listen to us, please. You're looking in the wrong place. Forget Lexington County. Look in Saluda County. Do you understand?"

Hilda: "Look in Saluda County?"

Kidnapper: "Exactly. Uh, closest to Lexington County within a fifteen-mile radius right over the line… is that understood?"

Hilda: "Yes."

Kidnapper: "Well, tell Sheriff Metts that he… I don't know what the problem is. I told you to forget about looking around your house… Saluda County."

Hilda: "Listen, there are so many people that love Shari, and they just won't give up."

Kidnapper: "I want to tell you one other thing. Shari is now a part of me physically, mentally, emotionally, and spiritually. Our souls are now one."

Hilda: "Your souls are one now with Shari?"

Kidnapper: "And she said she does love y'all, and like she said, do not let this ruin your lives… and well, time's up, and please now have the ambulance ready at any time."

Hilda: "Is her condition getting bad? Is that what you're trying to tell…"

Kidnapper: "Just have the ambulance, and I'll give you the location and tell Sheriff Metts to get all his damn men in Saluda County. Ok, well, God bless all of us."

Hilda: "Will you call me soon?"

Kidnapper: "I will. I've got to be careful. I've got to go now, and, and listen. Please, please, please forgive me for this. It just got out of hand."

Hilda: "Just tell Shari... I know she knows how much I love her. Tell her her Daddy loves her, and her brother and sister love her. God bless you for taking care of her."

Kidnapper: "Shari is protected, and like I said, she is a part of me now, and God looks after all of us. Goodnight."

Hilda: "Good luck to you, too."

Again, the call was traced but their efforts were fruitless. The call came from another pay phone eight miles from the Smiths' home. No clues at all were found at the pay phone.

By this time, several thousand volunteers were helping with the search. The family and Shari's boyfriend were heavily guarded inside the house and not allowed to leave without an officer with them.

The following evening – Tuesday, June 4 – the Smiths received another phone call at 9:45 p.m. Again, Dawn answered.

Dawn: "Hello."

Kidnapper: "Dawn?"

Dawn: "Yes."

Kidnapper: "This is Shari Faye's request. Have your mother get on the other phone quickly."

Dawn: "Get to the other phone, mother."

Kidnapper: "Get a pencil and paper ready."

Dawn: "Get a pencil and paper ready, ok. Mother's not on the phone yet."

Kidnapper: "Ok, now this is Shari's own words. So listen carefully. Say nothing unless you're asked. Ok, and I know these calls are taped and traced, but that's irrelevant now. There's no money demanded, so here's Shari Faye's last request. On the fifth day, to put the family at rest... Shari Faye being freed. Remember, we are one soul now. When located, you'll locate both of us together. We are one. God has chosen us. Respect all past and present requests. Actual events and times... jot this down."

Dawn: "All right, I'm doing it."

Kidnapper: "3:28 in the afternoon, Friday, thirty-first of May, Shari... Shari Faye was kidnapped from your mailbox with a gun. She had the fear of God in her, and she was at the mailbox. That's why she did not return back to her car."

Hilda: "Fear of God?"

Kidnapper: "Ok, 4:58 a.m.... no, I'm sorry. Hold on a minute. 3:10 a.m., Saturday, the first of June, uh, she handwrote what you received. 4:58 a.m., Saturday, the first of June... became one soul."

Hilda: "Became one soul. What does that mean?"

Kidnapper: "No questions now. Last, between four and seven Wednesday, tomorrow, have ambulance ready. Remember, no circus."

Hilda: "Wait, between four and seven a.m.?"

Kidnapper: "Four and seven in the afternoon tomorrow."

Hilda: "In the afternoon, ok."

Kidnapper: "Prayers and relief coming soon... please learn to enjoy life. Forgive. God protects the chosen. Shari Faye's important request... rest tonight and tomorrow. Good shall come out of this. Blessings are near. Remember tomorrow, Wednesday, four in the afternoon until seven in the evening. Ambulance ready... no circus."

Hilda: "No circus. What does that mean?"

Kidnapper: "You will receive last-minute instructions where to find us."

Hilda: "Do not kill my daughter, please. I mean, please."

Kidnapper: "We love and miss y'all. Get good rest tonight, goodbye."

Dawn: "He's gone, Mama."

Within minutes, police arrived at the pay phone that was used for the call, and again, no clues were useable. Police immediately set up roadblocks encircling the area of the pay phone, but after several hours of searching, there was still no sign of the kidnapper.

The following day, on Wednesday, June 5, at 11:54 a.m., the kidnapper called again. This time, Shari's mother, Hilda, answered. The call was extremely brief.

Hilda: "Hello."

Kidnapper: "Listen carefully. Take Highway 378 west to traffic circle. Take Prosperity exit, go one and a half miles, turn right at sign. Masonic Lodge Number 103, go one-quarter mile, turn left at white-framed building, go to back-yard. Six feet beyond. We're waiting. God chose us."

Police immediately raced from the Smiths' home to the location described in nearby Saluda County, about sixteen miles away. Shari's decomposing body was found lying on her back, exactly where he explained, in a wooded area directly behind the white building. There was no trace of the killer. She was still wearing the same clothes she wore when she was abducted, but a few pieces of jewelry were missing. There were remnants of duct tape attached to her face, and parts of her hair had been cut where the duct tape had been previously attached. The killer most likely knew that the duct tape could have left clues for the police.

Because of the extreme temperatures of over 100 degrees Fahrenheit during the past few days, her body was already decomposing rapidly, and there were signs of insect infestation. The medical examiner determined Shari had been dead for three to four days. Most likely, she had been killed within twelve hours of her abduction.

Determining the cause of death was a bit complicated. Because of Shari's rare form of diabetes, she most likely died of cardiac arrest caused by extreme dehydration. There were also signs of soft ligature strangulation or smothering. Either way, the medical examiner considered it a homicide,

"The findings present at the autopsy would fit with a number of causes of death. The two most likely causes are extreme dehydration with associated electrolyte imbalance causing cardiac arrest and asphyxia due to soft ligature strangulation or smothering. It is, therefore, my opinion, in light of the history of the case and the postmortem and autopsy findings, the cause of death best be left undetermined. As far as the manner of death, since the death occurred during abduction, the manner of death will still be homicide, regardless of whether it is due to depriving the decedent of water or from some type of homicidal asphyxia."

All previous calls had been placed near the Smiths' home, but the most recent call was placed over forty-five miles away in Saluda County. Police now believed he might be leaving the area, but that assumption changed when the killer called once again. This time, he called a local television reporter for Channel 10, Charlie Keyes. The killer explained that he wanted to turn himself in and be taken alive.

The killer tried to explain his actions. He wanted Keyes to contact Sheriff Metts and arrange for him to give himself up.

"…it just went bad. I know her family and her, and well, I just made a mistake. It went too far. All I wanted to do was to make love to her. I didn't know she had the rare disease, and it just got out of hand. I got scared, and I have to do the right thing, Charlie."

That same evening, at 8:57 p.m., the killer called the Smith home again. This time, he called collect (also known as a reverse charge call). He wanted to let them know how he killed Shari.

In a long and rambling call, the killer explained to Dawn that he had taken photos of Shari while she was standing at the mailbox. He also claimed to have another letter from Shari and that she was at peace when he killed her. He said he was a family friend. Then he explained how he raped and sodomized her before he took her life and wavered between turning himself in and suicide. Dawn and her mother did their best to try to keep him on the line while the police traced the call. What follows are a few excerpts from the long call:

———

Killer: "Ok, so this is going to have to be the way it is, and she said that uh, she wasn't scared… that she knew that she was going to be an angel, and if I took the latter choice that she suggested to me, that she would forgive me, but our God's going to be the major judgment, and she'll probably end up seeing me in heaven, not in hell. And that uh, she requests… now please remember this. Now, she requests that y'all be sure to take her hands and fold them on her stomach like she's praying."

———

Dawn: "But Shari was not afraid, and she didn't cry or anything?"

Killer: "No, she didn't do anything, and uh, can you handle it if I tell you how she died?"

Dawn: "Yes."

Killer: "Ok, now be strong, now."

Dawn: "Ok."

Killer: "She said you were strong. She told me all about the family and everything. We talked and… oh God… and I am a family friend. That's the sad part."

Dawn: "You are a family friend?"

Killer: "Yeah, and that is why I can't face y'all. You… you'll find out in the morning or tomorrow."

———

Killer: "Ok, I tied her up to the bedpost and uh, with electric cord, and uh, she didn't struggle, cry or anything. She let me voluntarily …(conversation missing)… from her chin to her head, ok, I'll go ahead and tell you. I took duct tape and wrapped it all the way around her head and suffocated her, and tell the coroner or get the information out how she died, and uh, I was unaware she had this disease. I probably would have never taken her, and uh, I shouldn't have took her anyway. It just got out of hand, and uh, I'd asked her out before, and she said she would if she wasn't going with anybody…."

———

Killer: Ok, now, are there any other questions? I've got to go now. Time's running out."

Dawn: "Uh, when… when you killed Shari, was she at peace? She wasn't afraid or anything?"

Killer: "She was not. She was at peace. She knew that God was with her, and she was going to become an angel."

Dawn: "And she wrote that letter to us of her own free will and all that was…."

Killer: "She sure did. Everything I've told y'all has been the truth. Hasn't everything come true?"

Dawn: "Yes, it has. Can… can I ask you one more question?"

Killer: "One more, and that's it."

Dawn: "You told us that Shari was kidnapped at gunpoint?"

Killer: "Yeah."

Dawn: "But she knew you?"

Killer: "Yeah. At first, see, I pulled up and uh, I'm telling you the truth. I have no reason to lie to y'all. I've always told you the truth, right?"

Dawn: "Right."

Killer: "Ok, and I had her... asked her to stand there and took two instant pictures."

Dawn: "You asked her to stand where?"

Killer: "At the mailbox with her car in the background. These pictures, detailed pictures will be with... with the letter that you receive. Since I'm out of town... probably not 'til Saturday. And Charlie Keyes will get a copy, and your family will get a copy, and it's addressed to you unless the mail holds it up."

Dawn: "So, she didn't realize that you were going to kidnap her?"

Killer: "That's exactly right.

———

Dawn: "...Why on the fifth day did she want us to find her? Why not..."

Killer: "I don't know. She just... she just said that. I don't know. I don't have any idea. I'm telling you exactly how she died, so she died of suffocation. And so... ok anything else?"

Dawn: "Why did you... why did you do that?"

Killer: "She... I gave her a choice... to shoot her or give her a drug overdose or suffocate her."

Dawn: "Why did you have to kill her?"

Killer: "It got out of hand. I got scared because, uh, only God knows, Dawn. I don't know why. God forgive me for this, I hope. And I got to straighten it out, or he'll send me to hell, and I'll be there the rest of my life, but I'm not going to be in prison and electric chair."

———

Killer: "Oh, yeah. Let me tell you. The other night, they almost caught me. The ignorant son-of-a-guns, I wanted them to catch me. I felt that way at the time, but now…."

Dawn: "When… when was this?"

Killer: "Uh, when I called at 9:45."

Dawn: "When you were over near Jake's Landing?"

Killer: "Yeah, I was at that Fast Fare thing."

Dawn: "Yeah."

Killer: "I pulled out twenty yards in front of two flashing lights."

Dawn: "What color car did you have?"

Killer: "They hit it dead on it, red, and they didn't even… Dawn, I can't get over this. Them ignorant so-and-sos didn't even turn around and follow me, and I cut right at that blinking light down there to go the back way on Old Cherokee Road. And there was a highway patrolman or somebody in front of me and pulled the car in front of me, and he let me turn right on Old Cherokee Road. Can you believe that?"

Dawn: "So, you really wanted to be caught?"

Killer: "At that time, but it's too late now."

Dawn: "What kind of car was it?"

Killer: "Oh, well, they came mighty damn close. Dawn, they're not going to catch me, and I can't give you information because I got to make it back in time, and they'll stop me before I get back if I tell you, but they're right, it was a red one, and I almost got caught three or four times."

Dawn: "Was it a red Jetta?"

Killer: "Dawn, that's irrelevant now. If I die now, or if I die at six o'clock in the morning, it's irrelevant. Well, listen, Dawn."

Dawn: "I really wish you would just think about not killing yourself."

————

Dawn then put her mother on the phone:

Hilda: "Listen, I want to ask you something."

Killer: "This just got out of hand. This got out of hand…."

Hilda: "All you had to do was let her go."

Killer: "I was scared. She, she, was dehydrating so damn bad."

Hilda: "You could have called me for medicine. I would have met you anywhere."

Killer: "Well, that's irrelevant now."

Hilda: "I mean, all you had to do was let her go. Such a beautiful young life…."

Killer: "I know that. That's why I have to join her now, hopefully, and uh, Mrs. Smith, please, uh, ok, well, that's it. I got to go."

Hilda: "Did she know you when you stopped?"

Killer: "Yeah, uh, I took two pictures, Instamatic of, I made her stand… well, before she knew I was going to kidnap her, I asked her to stand at the mailbox, and you'll see by the picture… her car door. I think there's about eight pictures…."

Hilda: "Do you know all of us or just Shari?"

Killer: "I know the whole family, unfortunately, that's why I can't face you.

———

Killer: "I know this might be selfish, but, uh, you all please, ask a special prayer for me? Your, your daughter said that she was not afraid, and she was strong-willed. She, uh, knew that she was going to heaven, was going to be an angel, and like I told Dawn, she was going to be singing like crazy, and when she said that, she was smiling."

Hilda: "Did you tell her you were going to kill her?"

Killer: "Yes, I did, and I gave her the choice, like, it's on the recording. I asked her if she wanted it to be drug overdose, shot or, uh, uh, suffocated, and she picked suffocation."

Hilda: "My God, how could you?"

Killer: "Well, forgive us, God."

Hilda: "Not us… you."

Killer: "God only knows why this happened. I don't know. It just got out of hand. Goodbye, Mrs. Smith."

(The full transcript is available in the appendix at the end of this book.)

———

Dawn was able to keep him on the phone for a long time in order to get as many details as possible so they could try and identify the killer.

The call originated fifty miles away in Great Falls, South Carolina. But again, no clues were found at the pay phone.

That Saturday, the Smith family held the funeral for Shari, and everyone in attendance was videotaped. Police believed the killer might show up. Shortly after the family returned home from the funeral, he called again and spoke to Dawn.

This time, he wanted to let her know that he was indeed at the funeral, and the police were too dumb to catch him. Again, he rambled on about killing himself, but Dawn took control of the conversation and put him on the defensive.

The killer tried to make it sound like he and Shari had become best friends. He claimed she was sharing all kinds of personal information with him, but Dawn wasn't falling for it. She was growing sick of him.

(The full transcript of this call is also available in the appendix at the end of this book.)

———

This time, the call was placed from Augusta, Georgia, about sixty miles away. As per usual, no traces were found at the pay phone.

FBI Profiler John Douglas was called in to provide a prospective profile of the killer. Douglas is now well-known for his work on Netflix's *Mindhunter* series, as well as for being one of the first criminal profilers. He has interviewed some of the worst killers in history, including Edmund Kemper, Ted Bundy, David Berkowitz, John Wayne Gacy, Charles Manson, Gary Ridgeway, and many others. Douglas' analysis came up with a suspect that would be in his late twenties to early thirties, single, a blue-collar worker, lived nearby, had low self-esteem, was overweight, had above-average intelligence, and had a prior criminal record. He also believed that the killer might work with electronics or phone systems because of the voice distortion device used on every call. He also believed the tone of the phone calls indicated that he was an asocial obsessive-compulsive. Finally, Douglas thought the killer felt a strong will to have a sense of power but had never experienced it until this time in his life.

Another week passed, and the killer had not been heard from. Police thought that maybe he had done as he'd hinted and taken his own life. However, exactly two weeks after Shari's abduction, the investigators' worst fears came true. At almost the exact same time of day, it happened again.

Roughly a thirty-minute drive from the Smith home, nine-year-old Debra May Helmick was playing in the front yard of her home with her three-year-old brother, Woody. Their father was just a few feet away inside their trailer home when a neighbor, Ricky Morgan, saw a silver car with red racing stripes drive up. A man got out of the vehicle, grabbed Debra May around the waist, and threw her in the car while she was kicking and screaming. The vehicle then sped away.

Debra May's father hadn't heard his daughter's screams because of the loud air conditioner running in the trailer but was alerted by Ricky Morgan, who had witnessed the abduction. Terrified, little three-year-old Woody only said, "The bad man said he was coming back to get me."

Debra Mae Helmick & Shari Smith

The two men got in their car and went in the direction the abductor's car was going, but they found nothing. Police immediately started an air and ground search. Their fear was that this was the same man that had killed Shari Smith.

Police now had a witness that could give a description not only of the car but of Debra May's kidnapper himself. Ricky Morgan described him as a thirty to thirty-five-year-old white male, approximately five-foot-nine, with a protruding stomach, a short beard and mustache, and brown hair. From this new information, police now drew up another sketch of the suspect.

Eight days had gone by, and there was no sign of Debra May. It had been fourteen days since the Smith family had heard from the killer when he called collect once again. Dawn retook the call, but this time he didn't want to talk about Shari,

Killer: "God wants you to join Shari Faye. It's just a matter of time... this month... next month... this year... next year. You can't be protected all the time... and you know... uh... have you heard about Debra May Hamrick [sic]?"

Dawn: "Uh, no."

Killer: "The ten-year-old... H-E-L-M-I-C-K."

Dawn: "Richland County?"

Killer: "Yeah, uh-huh, ok, now listen carefully... Go 1 north... well... Bill's Grill. Go three and a half miles through Gilbert. Turn right. Last dirt road before you come to stop sign at Two-Notch Road. Go through chain and no trespassing sign. Go fifty yards and to the left. Go ten yards. Debra May is waiting. God forgive us all."

Dawn: "Hey! Listen."

Killer: "What?"

Dawn: "Uh, just out of curiosity, how old are you?"

Killer: "Dawn E., your time is near. God forgive us and protect us all. Goodnight for now, Dawn E. Smith."

Dawn: "Wait a second here, what happened to the pictures you said you were gonna send me?"

Killer: "Apparently, the FBI must have them."

Dawn: "No, sir, because when they have something, we get it too, you know. Are you gonna send them? I think you're jerking me around because you said they were coming, and they're not here."

Killer: "Dawn E. Smith, I must go."

Dawn: "Listen, you said you were gonna... and you did not give me those photos."

Killer: "Goodnight, Dawn, I'll talk to you later."

The killer was clearly now fixated on Dawn. He was now threatening her by calling her "Dawn E. Smith" and telling her that she would soon join her sister.

Police raced to the location given. In the bushes, they found the decomposed body of the tiny, blonde girl. She was clothed in her tank top, shorts, and panties, but over her panties were a pair of silk adult bikini briefs. Like Shari, remnants of duct tape were found in her hair.

Again, the unusually warm temperatures that summer had accelerated the decomposition, and an autopsy was inconclusive. An official cause of death could not be determined, but suffocation was presumed. It also could not be determined if the girl had been raped, though the odd extra pair of panties suggested she had. A pink barrette found near the body with a clump of blonde hair was shown to Mrs. Helmick. She confirmed that it belonged to Debra May.

As expected, the trace of the call resulted in no evidence. The killer was long gone by the time police arrived; there were no witnesses, and the phone had been wiped clean of fingerprints.

Police now worried that the killer had no intention of stopping and that Dawn was going to be the next victim.

Luckily, the forensic document team would soon get their most significant break. The "Last Will and Testament" letter that had been mailed to the family revealed more clues.

Forensic document examiners were able to recover an imprint of a partial phone number from the letter and the name "Joe." The phone number was a Huntsville, Alabama prefix, and the last four digits were only missing one digit, leaving only ten possible phone numbers.

Police called all ten numbers until they found someone with the name Joe. One of the numbers belonged to a young man named Joey Sheppard. When they searched the phone records of Joey Sheppard, they found that he had received calls from a phone in Saluda County, where Shari's body was found.

When investigators called Joey Sheppard, he was quickly eliminated as a suspect. He didn't fit the FBI profile. They asked him if he knew anyone in Lexington or Saluda counties, and he replied, "Yes, my parents live in Saluda County."

On the evening of June 26, police raced to the home of Ellis and Sharon Sheppard, just two miles from where Shari's body was found. They were expecting to find their suspect but were quickly disappointed. The Sheppards didn't fit the FBI profile either.

Detectives decided to question the Sheppards and found that they had just returned from a six-week trip. They explained that they often traveled for extended periods, and a local man that worked for Ellis, Larry Gene Bell, would house-sit for them.

They described Larry Gene Bell as a mid-thirties white male who lived with his parents and had reddish-brown hair, a beard, and a mustache. The description fit the FBI profile perfectly.

Detectives questioned the Sheppards all night until the early morning the next day. During the questioning, they played the tapes of the phone calls for the Sheppards. Despite the electronic distortion of the calls, the Sheppards quickly confirmed that it was the voice of Larry Gene Bell.

Larry Gene Bell

They told police that Bell had picked them up from the airport just a few days earlier, when they returned from their vacation. The conversation on the drive home from the airport was dominated by the news of the two murders. Bell seemed to be obsessed with the murders. Mrs. Sheppard mentioned that Bell had mistakenly called her "Shari" on several occasions since they returned from their trip. He had also collected all of the news articles of the murders from the local newspapers. All of this fit the FBI profile of the suspected killer.

Bell had been staying at the Sheppards' home while they were on vacation, so police searched the house. They found that Ellis' .38 caliber handgun was missing.

Bell was due to come to the Sheppards' home that morning at 7:30 a.m. to work. Police arrested Bell as he left his home on the morning of June 27.

After Bell's arrest, a forensic team continued their search of the Sheppards' home. They found Mr. Sheppard's missing .38 revolver underneath the mattress in the bedroom where he had been staying. They also found a blonde hair that DNA later proved was from Shari Smith.

During the interrogations of Larry Gene Bell, he admitted nothing. Hilda and Dawn Smith even came in to try and entice him to confess, but he just mumbled nonsensically and said,

"…this Larry Gene Bell couldn't have done this, but another Larry Bell could have been the one."

Hilda told him that she knew he'd killed her daughter, but she didn't hate him. Bell teared up but still didn't confess.

Bell made a mockery of the trial, blurting out strange comments, refusing to answer questions, and rambling and mumbling nonsense. One of his favorite responses to questioning was, "Silence is Golden," and at one point, he yelled, "I would like Dawn E. Smith to marry me!"

Larry Gene Bell was found guilty of murdering both Shari Smith and Debra May Helmick and sentenced to death. During his incarceration, he repeatedly claimed that he was Jesus Christ.

Bell chose to die by the electric chair rather than lethal injection and was put to death on October 4, 1996.

CHAPTER 5
A UNICORN AMONG BEASTS

L ife on the Hawaiian island of Maui is very relaxed. The North Shore of Maui, where the big waves can be found, attracts surfers, beach bums, hippies, and people who just love to enjoy life. Carly "Charli" Scott was one of those people.

Charli was a fun-loving girl who lived near the North Shore and loved the laid-back lifestyle of Maui. With her pin-up girl looks, Charli was known for her quirkiness, taste in music, clothes, and bright red hair. She loved to sing out loud and often went out of her way to help her friends and family.

Charli moved to Maui from Woodland, California, in 2004. Even in her twenties, Charli still had a child-like side to her. She was fascinated with unicorns, and her favorite movie was 1982's "The Last Unicorn." She often quoted the Chinese philosopher You Rou, saying she was a "unicorn among beasts." Unfortunately, the beast she met was named Steven Capobianco.

Steven Capobianco met Charli in 2009, when she was twenty-two years old, and he was just nineteen. Charli was smitten with Steven, and the couple moved in together in the town of Kula, just a few miles upcountry from the beach town of Paia. Though they lived together for two full years, Steven often told his friends they were just roommates, even going so far as to avoid having his picture taken with her.

Though Charli openly loved Steven, that love was not reciprocated. Steven never told her he loved her, and according to her friends, he never showed her any affection at all other than sex.

Charli had a motherly side to her as well. She enjoyed making Steven's life comfortable by cooking and cleaning the house, while Steven spent hours in front of the television playing video games or working on his truck. Though the couple lived together, they didn't do many activities together. To their friends' knowledge, Steven was never abusive to her, but behind her back, he would tell his friends, "I hate that fucking bitch."

Steven Capobianco & Charli Scott

When Steven and Charli inevitably broke up, they still had an on-again-off-again relationship for the next few years.

Charli was still in love, even though she knew Steven didn't care about her, while Steven knew Charli was always there if he needed her for sex. No matter how badly Steven treated her, Charli was under his spell and just couldn't seem to say "no." She came running every time he called.

In the fall of 2013, Steven met a young blonde named Cassandra Kupstas, and the two started dating. Cassandra claimed it was "love at first sight." She was living on Maui when she met Steven but already had plans to move back to her hometown in Pennsylvania.

Though they only had three weeks together before she moved 5,000 miles away, they fell very much in love. Once Cassandra returned to Pennsylvania, she and Steven spoke on the phone via Skype twice a day. She had only been back for a few days before they both realized that they needed to be together, so they made plans for her to move back to Maui the following February.

Neither Steven nor Cassandra seemed to be the faithful type. Early on in their relationship, Steven learned that Cassandra had cheated on him, so he decided to go to a bar in the town of Makawao to drown his sorrows. Steven ran into Charli at the bar. Charli lent a sympathetic ear and invited him over to her place. As usual, Steven was only interested in sex, and Charli knew she couldn't resist.

The cheating was just a minor setback for Steven and Cassandra, as they quickly patched up their relationship and continued with their plans of creating a life together.

That October, just over a month after their hookup, Charli realized she was pregnant. Although this wasn't the ideal situation, Charli had always looked forward to the idea of being a mother.

When Charli told Steven the news, he was less than pleased and told her he wanted to take a paternity test to ensure he was the father. Unfortunately, this pregnancy got directly in the way of Steven's plans with his new love, Cassandra.

He told Charli he wouldn't be there for her baby and insisted she get an abortion. Charli reluctantly agreed, and the two went to Planned Parenthood for a consultation.

During their visit, the director of the local Planned Parenthood noticed the tension between the couple and asked Steven if he was the father. Steven replied,

"I guess so... but she's not with me."

The director looked at Charli and saw an unmistakable look of pain on her face. Steven then blurted out,

"We're going to go through with this, aren't we?"

Charli agreed, and they made plans for Charli to come back later for the procedure.

———

Christmas dinner was held at the home of Charli's half-sister, Fiona, and Charli thought this was the perfect time to announce to her family that she was now three months pregnant and having a baby.

Charli hadn't spoken to Steven since their appointment at Planned Parenthood and had since changed her mind. She'd decided to keep the baby and raise it on her own – with or without Steven's help. She knew that no matter what her situation, she would always have the support of her family and friends.

Jaws dropped, and mouths were wide open around the room. Charli's family was shocked but ultimately overjoyed for her when they saw how excited she was. She had already learned the gender of the baby and had decided she would name him Joshua.

Her half-sister Fiona was curious if Steven knew about the baby, so she sent him a text, "Do you realize you are the father of Charli's child?" Steven replied, "What? How do you know? I thought she had taken care of it?" He had no idea that Charli had changed her mind and decided to keep the baby.

When Fiona spoke to Steven on the phone later that day, he sounded nervous and panicked. He couldn't believe the news. He said that he and Charli had agreed to "take care of it." He told her he had a new girlfriend that he loved, and she was moving in with him in February. However, he worried that this baby would mess up his plans. He ended the conversation by saying, "I need to talk to Charli."

A few weeks had passed before Steven worked up the nerve to break the news to Cassandra during their daily Skype sessions. Steven explained that he didn't know for sure that the baby was his, and he had asked Charli to have an abortion, having even taken her to the clinic himself.

Cassandra, however, was in shock. At only twenty-one years old, she wasn't ready to be a stepmother and told Steven she didn't want to talk for a few days while she processed the news.

Eventually, Cassandra called Steven and told him she didn't want him to be a deadbeat dad and that he should take responsibility for the child. She said he should be there for his son, but she could sense that Steven still wasn't ready to become a father. He told Cassandra he had no feelings for Charli and had never had any feelings for her, explaining "she was just an easy lay."

On the evening of Sunday, February 9, Charli, her mother, and her four sisters gathered at her sister Brooke's house for a relaxed evening watching Disney videos. Brooke had recently found out she was pregnant too, and they talked about their children growing up together on Maui. Brooke later recalled feeling her sister's tummy as Joshua was kicking.

Around 8:00 p.m. that evening, Charli kissed her mother, told her she loved her, and made her way home. Sadly, it was the last time any of her family saw her.

———

Charli lived only a few miles away from her mother and planned to drop laundry with her on her way to the Hui No'eau Visual Arts Center in nearby Makawao, where she worked as an administrator.

But when Charli didn't show up that morning, her mother, Kimberlyn, called her cell phone. She wasn't surprised when Charli didn't answer. Charli should have been at work by then and typically didn't answer personal calls while working. Kimberlyn then sent her a text message, knowing Charli would respond when she had the time.

As the day progressed, Charli's mother sent a few more texts but received no reply each time. Charli was a very responsible girl, and it was unusual for her to not reply. That was when Kimberlyn started getting worried. By 4:00 p.m., she had already sent her daughter several messages and eventually sent one saying, "Where the hell are you?" By 9:00 p.m., Kimberlyn and the rest of the family were in full-on panic mode.

That evening, Kimberlyn and Charli's sixteen-year-old sister, Phaedra, went to Charli's house. Her Toyota 4Runner wasn't parked outside, and the doors to her home were locked. They knocked, knowing there would be no answer. However, they could hear one of her dogs inside the house. They had keys, so they let themselves in.

Upon entering the house, they found one of Charli's dogs, Zoey, with no dog food or water. Charli would never have left her dogs without food and water. Unfortunately, her second dog, Nala, was missing.

Kimberlyn then remembered that she and Charli shared an app called Life360 that was used for families to track the location of one another, specifically in situations like this. When she checked the app, it showed that the last ping from Charli's phone was at 10:56 p.m. the night before in Ke'anae.

Ke'anae was a remote area along Maui's North Shore, just a short distance from the famous road to Hana. It was a beautiful peninsula with huge waves that crashed against the jagged black rocks of the shoreline, but there was no explainable reason why Charli would have gone there – particularly that late at night when she was five months pregnant.

As the family hypothesized about why Charli would have possibly been that far out in the middle of the night, only one reason came to mind. There was only one person that Charli would see without telling anyone: Steven Capobianco.

At 10:19 p.m. Monday night, Kimberlyn sent Charli one last text, "I'm about to call the police, Charli. Where are you???"

When there was still no answer, she called Maui Police and reported Charli missing.

Maui Police showed up at Steven Capobianco's house at 5:30 Monday morning to question him. But he seemed surprised; he claimed it was the first he had heard of Charli's disappearance.

Steven told detectives that Charli had come to his house on Sunday night because he'd asked for a ride to pick up his truck. He said the battery cable had come loose as he drove on the road to Hana the previous day, and he'd left his truck parked on the side of the road. He needed a ride to the truck so he could repair the cable and drive it home. He explained that the vehicle had been stalled just a few miles past Ke'anae at mile marker twenty. It was the exact location where Charli's cell phone last pinged the tracking app.

According to Steven, Charli drove him to his truck that night, and she didn't even need to get out of her vehicle. He claimed she shined her headlights on his truck while he fixed the battery cable and the whole process only took a few minutes. They then drove back toward town in their own vehicles. Steven said Charli followed him on the way back, but he drove faster than she did and lost sight of her headlights near Ulalena Loop in the Twin Falls area, just twenty minutes from her home.

Steven explained that he sent her a text when he got home to thank her, but he didn't receive a reply.

———

Tuesday at daybreak, the entire family gathered with friends and began their search of the island. They hoped they would find that Charli had rolled her car off the side of the road to Hana and just couldn't get help.

Search crews scoured up and down the road to Hana. They thought she could be anywhere between Haiku and Hana, a forty-mile stretch of twists and turns, one-lane bridges, and sharp cliffs on the ocean side of the road. They were looking for skid marks, broken railings, broken bushes, or any sort of clue at all. By nightfall, however, they'd found nothing.

That evening, friends and family posted on Facebook, and the local news stations picked up the story. Word spread fast around the island that Charli was missing. Just a month prior, another Maui woman, Moreira "Mo" Monsalve, had mysteriously disappeared. Speculation quickly spread that the two cases may have been related.

Wednesday morning, there was a clue. Charli's other dog, Nala, had been found at the Nāhiku Marketplace, an area much further towards Hana. Nāhiku was eight miles past where Steven said his truck broke down and about twenty-five miles from where he said he lost sight of Charli's head-lights that night.

The man who found Nala said he found her wandering around Nāhiku Marketplace on Monday morning. Her hair wasn't dirty, and her paws seemed clean and not cracked. Police knew that if a dog had traveled any distance in the rugged area, it would have matted hair and muddy or cracked paws. So, while it was good news that Nala was found safe, it also presented more significant problems. Her family knew that Charli would never willingly leave Nala alone. Also, it left the question of how Nala got that far down the Hana Highway without getting dirty. Someone had to have dropped her off way out there.

That same afternoon, searchers found Charli's vehicle. Her 1997 Toyota 4Runner was located near the famous surf spot, Jaws: it was flipped on its side, completely burned. Forensic experts found the use of accelerants on the passenger side and the rear of the SUV. Everything that wasn't metal had been burned and completely disintegrated. Police questioned two nearby families who said they smelled the toxic smoke burning throughout the night.

Charli's father and several other relatives and friends flew out from the mainland. They all came to help with the search. Local Maui residents came from all over the island to help, donating their horses, search dogs, and helicopters, but families and searchers had a sinking feeling that the chances of finding Charli alive were slim.

On Thursday, a search team found a pair of jeans with bloodstains thrown alongside the Hana Highway. The size matched Charli's, and later analysis showed the blood was hers. Investigators also found a single hair in the pocket of the jeans. DNA taken from the hair was later found to match that of Steven Capobianco.

Late Thursday afternoon, Charli's younger sister, Phaedra, thought it would be best to thoroughly search the Ke'anae area near Nua'ailua Bay, since it was the last ping location of Charli's cell phone. As she and Brooke drove down the road to the area of Paraquat's Beach, they saw lights coming up the dirt road. They instantly recognized them as the headlights of Steven Capobianco's truck. Steven stopped them as they drove down the secluded dirt road and told them he had already searched that area and found nothing. He offered to search the area again with them, but Phaedra and Brooke felt uneasy being alone with him. Instead, they decided to return home and search the area later.

Another of Charli's friends, Adam Gaines, heard a similar story from Steven earlier that day.

Late that evening, when they knew Steven wasn't in the area anymore, Phaedra took two friends back to the area near Paraquat's Beach to do their own search.

The brush in the area was very thick, so the three of them used flashlights and spread out wide enough to where they could still hear each other. Just a few feet into the brush, Phaedra found something. It was a DVD of the movie Twilight. That DVD had been in Charli's car when she went missing.

As they searched deeper into the woods, Molly Wirth found a long black skirt and a blue polka-dot tank top. These were the clothes Charli was wearing on Sunday night, when they saw her last. The skirt, however, had at least 20 puncture marks concentrated around the abdomen area.

As they continued their search, they came to a stream and were overwhelmed by a horrible stench. Something was rotten and decomposing. A green blanket covered with maggots lay on the banks of the stream. It was a blanket that Charli had kept in her vehicle. Nearby were a pair of Perry Ellis jeans, a gray hoodie, and two rolls of masking tape. Terrified at what they had found, the three returned home and contacted Maui Police.

At daybreak, investigators began a full forensic search of the area near Nua'ailua Bay. During their extensive search, they recovered a black bra with cuts in it, five fingernails, skin fragments, clumps of red hair, a body piercing with flesh still attached to it, a bone fragment, and two halves of a lower jawbone. DNA analysis matched them all to Charli Scott.

Forensic analysis of the jawbone showed it was split into two pieces and had marks of dismemberment, blunt force trauma, and removal of flesh with a serrated edge.

Although the search for more body parts continued, it was now clear that Charli had been brutally murdered. The case was now considered a homicide.

Maui prosecutors took their time building their case against Steven Capobianco. Initially, he was only listed as a person of interest – not officially a suspect. During this time, Steven was cocky and convinced he wouldn't be arrested. He spoke with reporters, repeating his story. He said he took a lie detector test but was told he'd failed,

> "They didn't make me take it again. I'm honestly not convinced I failed; I think they might have just said that as a tactic, but I really don't know. I'm walking around right now without handcuffs on."

Four months after finding the jawbone, Maui Police arrested Steven Capobianco for Charli Scott's murder. He was charged with second-degree murder and third-degree arson. Almost every part of Steven's story fell apart as the evidence piled up against him.

Though much of the evidence against Steven was largely circumstantial, his story's sheer volume of inconsistencies was monumental.

The FBI analyzed his cell phone usage: when he claimed his truck had broken down on the road to Hana, his cell phone was actually being used over twenty miles away in Haiku, near his home.

Steven claimed that his friend, Kyle Knight, had picked him up the following morning and given him a ride to work, but Kyle told investigators that was a lie. Security video near his work showed him driving his truck that morning at 6:41 – the same time he claimed the truck was broken down on Hana Highway. That same day, a coworker told detectives he had retrieved a backpack from Steven's truck, parked in the parking lot at his work.

Even Steven's grandfather testified that he left the house that morning in his own truck.

At the trial, local residents who traveled the road to Hana every day testified that they didn't see any vehicles broken down that morning. Steven's story for why the truck broke down didn't make sense, either. If the battery cable had come loose while the vehicle was running, the engine would still run until it was turned off.

Steven made another crucial mistake during interviews with the police and television reporters. He mistakenly referred to Charli in the past tense, before any body parts had been found.

Perhaps his most incriminating inconsistencies were the three different stories he gave for why his hands were injured.

Capobianco had a Skype conversation with his girlfriend, Cassandra, at 2:30 a.m. on Monday, just hours after Charli disappeared. Cassandra told investigators he acted nervous and frantic. He showed Cassandra his scratched and bloody hands and claimed he'd smashed one hand on the hood of a friend's car, then a battery terminal had sliced the other. During the trial, Cassandra testified,

"He was kind of frantic and wound up, like someone who had just got out of a car accident."

The following morning, referring to the same injury, he told a coworker at Mana Foods that he'd injured his hand working on the window of a friend's car. He claimed the cable that pulls the window up had wrapped around his hand, and he'd lost feeling in it. However, experts testified during the trial that the Honda window cable he referred to was encased in an enclosure that would have made it impossible for the cable to wrap around his hand.

During a police interrogation, Steven told Detective Loo that he had injured his hands at Mana Foods, where he worked as a baker. He also said he'd sliced his pinky while working on the window of his truck, not a friend's car.

Everything about Steven's story was a lie and cell phone data put him in the exact remote location of Charli's death. How she was killed, however, is still a mystery.

———

On December 28, 2016, a jury returned with a guilty verdict on both counts after twenty-eight days of deliberation. Steven Capobianco was sentenced to life in prison without the possibility of parole.

During his incarceration, Capobianco's aunt, Susan Capobianco, was arrested when visiting Steven at Maui Community Correctional Center. She was caught trying to pass him a package that contained twelve cigarettes, 0.3 grams of methamphetamine, marijuana, hash oil, and rolling papers. She was sentenced to eighteen months in jail and four years of probation.

CHAPTER 6
THE CANAL KILLER

In the late 1700s, London was growing rapidly, and merchants needed a way to get goods to the seagoing ships on the River Thames. A vast series of canals and locks were built throughout the city to bring goods to the Thames using small canal boats. Those canals still exist today, though they are no longer used for trade. Today, the canals offer a peaceful place for walkers, runners, boaters, cyclists, and tourists to enjoy away from the city traffic.

Regent's Canal was built in 1812 and is still one of the most beautiful canals in London. It stretches over eight miles from Paddington to the Thames, encircling the heart of the city. The canal banks are very popular and usually quite busy.

On an afternoon in February 2001, two boys were fishing in Regent's Canal when one of their lines got caught on something on the bottom of the canal. When the boys reeled in the line, they found that it had snagged a duffel bag. They managed to drag the bag to the canal's edge but needed help getting it onto the bank.

Curious, the boys unzipped the bag and found it filled with bricks and ceramic tiles. However, there was also something wrapped tightly with plastic. They opened the plastic and were hit with the sharp stench of decomposition. When they called the London police, investigators confirmed that it was a human body part.

Police were sent in to dredge the canal. Divers found five additional duffel bags, each filled with bricks and each containing more body parts. Six bags were found in total, with ten body parts. The torso had been cut in half, the legs were cut at the hips and knees, and the arms were severed at the shoulders and elbows. The head, hands, and feet were all missing.

An autopsy revealed that the body was female, but not much forensic evidence was available. Bloodwork was sent to the lab, and through DNA, they were able to find out who she was. She was in the system for drug offenses and prostitution.

The body belonged to thirty-one-year-old Paula Fields. Paula was a mother of three who was originally from Liverpool. She had moved to London to try to better her life but became addicted to crack cocaine and turned to prostitution after social services had taken her children away from her.

Police discovered that Paula had been dating a man named Joe Johnson four months earlier. However, they found no record of Joe Johnson, though he had a roommate named Tony Sweeney, who had a lengthy police record. Tony Sweeney's brother, John, also had a record and had been wanted for the attempted murder of his girlfriend in 1994. Before long, investigators realized that Joe Johnson was actually the fugitive John Sweeney.

Forensic analysis of soil found in the duffel bags proved it was identical to the soil from Sweeney's garden, where he lived on Digby Crescent in London. But that wasn't nearly enough to convict him of the murder of Paula Fields.

———

John Sweeney had been on the run from police for almost seven years, using different names wherever he went. He was working as a carpenter on a construction site in Central London when he was arrested on March 23, 2001.

The Many Faces of John Sweeney

Sweeney was arrested for the attempted murder of his former girlfriend, Delia Balmer, almost seven years earlier in 1994. Still, police hoped they could also gather enough evidence to link him to the murder of Paula Fields.

———

At the time of his arrest in 2001, Delia Balmer was still living in London and working as a nurse. She originally met John Sweeney in a London pub in 1991. They had dated and traveled throughout Europe and eventually decided to share a flat in London. However, the relationship soured over time as Sweeney became increasingly aggressive and possessive. By 1994, Delia had decided it was time to end the relationship and changed the locks on their home, but Sweeney didn't take kindly to that.

When Delia walked home from work, Sweeney followed close behind in the shadows. As she opened her door, he ran up behind her and pushed her over the threshold and into the apartment. He held her captive for seven full days. During that time, he tied her to the bed, repeatedly beat her, raped her, and threatened to cut out her tongue if she screamed.

When Delia's friends from work came to her house, they knew someone was inside, but no one would come to the door. Knowing something was wrong, they called the Kentish Town police.

When police arrived on November 14, 1994, Sweeney had Delia open the door ever so slightly while he hid behind the door. The officers could tell by Delia's demeanor that something was terribly wrong and forced the door open. Delia ran out of the door and into the street while police pushed their way in and arrested Sweeney for assault, rape, and unlawful confinement.

Inside, they found evidence that Sweeney had plans to kill Delia and dispose of her body. Sweeney had a "murder kit" containing plastic ground sheeting, orange rubber gloves, rolls of tape, a saw, a bow knife, and a box cutter knife.

Delia told police that while Sweeney had her tied up, he told her that he had murdered his prior girlfriend, Melissa, in Amsterdam. He said she was an American, and he had walked in on her having sex with two German men. He told her that he shot all three of them, sat with their dead bodies for several days, and then dismembered them and dumped them in the canals of Amsterdam. Sweeney taunted Delia, telling her that if she was a good girl then she wouldn't end up like Melissa.

Also inside the flat, police found several firearms and hundreds of paintings and poetry Sweeney had created. Both the artwork and the poetry were violent, dark, and graphic, with images of bloody, dismembered bodies and women being tortured. The poetry seemed to be a confession of his mayhem. One poem read:

> "Poor old Melissa
>
> Chopped her up in bits
>
> Food to feed the fish
>
> Amsterdam was the pits"

Police now suspected that Sweeney was a serial killer who had murdered at least one other girl in the same way that Paula Fields was murdered. London police contacted Amsterdam police, but they had no record of a murder matching their inquiry.

Unfortunately, Sweeney was released on bail after only a month in jail for his assault on Delia Balmer, but she wasn't notified of his release. Sweeney wasn't to go near Delia under the terms of his bail, but that didn't stop him. Within hours of his release, he was hiding near Delia's door again, waiting for her to return home from work.

As she approached her front door, Sweeney savagely attacked her with a knife and an axe, slashing her chest and cutting off one of her fingers. Luckily, a neighbor heard her screams, grabbed a baseball bat, and hit Sweeney across the back. Sweeney ran from the scene, and Delia barely escaped with her life. Her arms were broken, her lung was punctured, and her chest was permanently scarred.

———

Sweeney went on the run using several aliases and remained undetected by police until his arrest in 2001, after Paula Fields' body was found.

Though police didn't have enough evidence to prove that John Sweeney had butchered Paula Fields and dumped her in Regent's Canal, they had enough to get him into prison while they searched for more evidence. Sweeney was sentenced to serve nine years in prison for the attempted murder of Delia and firearms charges. With Sweeney behind bars, it gave investigators time to find more evidence in the Paula Fields case.

While Amsterdam authorities couldn't find any information about bodies dumped in the canals, they did, however, find something about an American girl named Melissa Halstead. She was reported missing in April 1990 by her family, but unfortunately, they had no more information on her.

———

Melissa Halstead was a rebellious young American girl who had dated Sweeney in the late eighties. She was a beautiful girl who had worked as a model for Ford Modeling in New York, then moved to London where she took up photography. She and Sweeney had a tumultuous relationship with frequent, violent arguments. On one occasion, he threw a chair at her, which permanently scarred her face. Still, no matter what he did, she always seemed to forgive him.

In 1988, Melissa was deported from the United Kingdom for working without a permit. She left Sweeney and moved to Vienna, Austria. Sweeney followed her, broke into the apartment she shared with a roommate, tied up her roommate, and searched the apartment for evidence that she had another lover. Later that day, he hunted her down and beat her with a clawhammer.

Sweeney was jailed for six months for the attack, but despite the abuse, Melissa again stayed with him. They moved throughout Europe to Stuttgart, Milan, and ultimately settled in Amsterdam. The relationship was still in constant turmoil, and Melissa told her sister that, if she ever went missing, John Sweeney had killed her. Eventually it happened. By April 1990, Melissa Halstead had disappeared.

———

Although Sweeney was imprisoned in March 2002 for the attempted murder of Delia Balmer, it was only temporary. He would soon be eligible for parole and potentially on the street before they found more evidence on the Melissa Halstead or Paula Fields cases. In 2004, the death of Paula Fields became a cold case.

———

In 2007, six years after Paula Fields' body parts were found, the London police got a call from the Rotterdam cold case investigation team. They were investigating all of their unsolved cases from 1990 onward.

On May 3, 1990, Rotterdam police had pulled several duffel bags from the Westersingel Canal in Rotterdam. Like Paula Fields, the bags had been weighted down with bricks and contained several dismembered female body parts. The head, hands, and feet were missing.

The Rotterdam team had already spoken to the police in Amsterdam and suspected they were the remains of Melissa Halstead. Melissa had been reported missing just one month before Rotterdam had originally found the body parts. It seemed that, after almost eighteen years, they could identify the body.

In January of 2008, just as time was running out and Sweeney would soon be eligible for parole, Amsterdam, Rotterdam, and London police worked together to exhume the remains of the unidentified body parts from 1990. Using the DNA of her relatives eighteen years after she had been reported missing, Dutch detectives confirmed the dismembered girl was Melissa Halstead.

Despite there being no forensic evidence against Sweeney, the similarities in the cases were all too familiar. On April 26, 2009, John Sweeney was removed from his cell and interviewed. He was officially charged with the murders of Paula Fields and Melissa Halstead, but he made no comment.

During the trial, prosecutors showed the jury his artwork and poetry. There were over 200 images, many depicting severed body parts similar to how the real body parts were found. One painting showed a man with a knife raised above his head, preparing to stab a woman. The caption read, "A romantic weekend for two in Austria." Another showed a female body with its hands, feet, and head cut off.

One of the most damning paintings was an image of Melissa Halstead. Next to her head was a gravestone; the text on the gravestone was covered with white correction fluid. Forensic investigators used ultraviolet light to look behind that correction fluid. He was trying to hide the writing on the gravestone, which read:

RIP

Melissa Holstead [sic]

Born 7 12 56

Died –

Yet another one of his paintings was a self-portrait, where he had a bloody axe tucked into his belt. While he sat in prison, he created several additional paintings with dismembered women's bodies cut up in the same manner as Paula and Melissa.

(Images of John Sweeney's artwork can be found in the online appendix at the end of this book.)

Sweeney often yelled at the prosecution during his trial, arguing that his paintings were random nonsense and abstract. He claimed many were made while he was tripping on LSD and weren't meant to be taken as realistic.

The jury, however, found his paintings and poetry to be confessions to the murders. After ten hours of deliberation, the jury returned with a guilty verdict.

On April 5, 2011, John Sweeney was sentenced to a "whole-life tariff," meaning he would spend the rest of his life in prison without the possibility of parole. The sentence was extremely rare in the United Kingdom, with less than 100 prisoners serving a whole-life tariff.

Prosecutors also believed that Sweeney may have been responsible for the disappearance of several more girls, including a Brazilian named Irani, a Columbian named Maria, and a nurse from Derbyshire, England, named Sue. During his incarceration, Sweeney described them as some of his (thirty to forty) girlfriends that police have been unable to locate.

CHAPTER 7
THE HEAD IN THE BUCKET

I n April 2001, Melanie Ovalle walked into a Vancouver, Canada, police station and told officers she needed to talk to someone about a murder. The young woman had a story that was a bit hard to believe, and the detectives assigned to her case didn't know what to make of it.

Melanie was a divorcee who lived with her mother, and from the outset, she admitted to detectives that she was bipolar and had been hanging around local drug dealers. For the police, that didn't help her story's credibility. The detectives knew that people who suffer from bipolar disorder could sometimes have lapses in perception, so what she explained to them might not be the actual truth. Despite their assumptions, Melanie gave a very detailed and persuasive story.

———

Melanie explained that her best friend, Lee-Ann Price, had shown up at her door three weeks earlier, crying hysterically. Lee-Ann said she had been driving around Vancouver with her boyfriend, Mihaly Illes. While he was driving, Illes repeatedly reached for something in the rear of his van. Finally, he grabbed a white Home Depot bucket just behind his seat. Out of curiosity, Lee-Ann looked into the bucket to see what inside it was so interesting to him, but what she saw shocked her to her core. Inside the bucket was a severed human head.

Melanie explained that Lee-Ann showed up at her house again the following day. This time, she brought her boyfriend with her. Melanie had previously met Illes and his associates, Derrick Madinsky and Javan Dowling, at a bar they frequented.

Mihaly Illes was well-known in certain circles throughout Vancouver as a drug dealer. He was a Hungarian national who had been deported from Canada several times for drug and weapons charges but somehow managed to always get back into the country illegally. He ran an elaborate operation that involved taking marijuana grown in British Columbia over the border into the United States. One pound of the highly potent "B.C. bud" that sold for $1,500 in Canada sold for more than $6,000 in Los Angeles. The DEA estimated that, at the time, the trafficking of Canadian marijuana into the United States was a billion-dollar industry.

But rather than selling the weed for cash, they exchanged it for crack cocaine which they would then smuggle back into Canada. This amplified their earnings exponentially. It was believed that Illes and his friends, Derrick Madinsky, Garry Favell, and Javan Dowling, were making more than $80,000 per deal.

Melanie was shocked when Lee-Ann arrived at her door with Illes in tow. She was terrified when Mihaly insisted that the three of them go for a drive. Mihaly was known as a violent man, and Melanie worried he might hurt her if she didn't go with them.

Melanie rode with them to a garage. Once inside, she recognized another of Illes' associates, Derrick Madinsky. Madinsky was busy cleaning the inside of a van.

Illes suddenly became agitated and pulled Melanie aside. In an attempt to intimidate her, he told her that he wanted to show her what happened to people who betrayed him. He then opened the Home Depot bucket and pulled out the human head. Right away, Melanie recognized the face. It was the head of twenty-seven-year-old Javan Dowling, another drug dealer on Illes' team.

Illes claimed Dowling was addicted to crack and had been skimming from their product. As a result, he had blown a deal with one of their most important clients, and Illes needed to prove to the client that he could take care of the situation. Illes also disapproved of him being homosexual. To make matters worse, Dowling had been living in an upscale high-rise suite in downtown Vancouver's Wall Centre, and Illes didn't like that he lived such an extravagant lifestyle.

––––––

Melanie continued her story and told detectives that Illes demanded she store the head in her garage. She didn't want to, but she was scared of him and felt she had no choice. That night, Illes moved the bucket with the severed head to Melanie's house and placed it in her garage. She wasn't sure why he wanted the head stored in her garage but assumed it was to make her believe she would be an accessory to the crime.

Illes and Lee-Ann showed up again the next day at Melanie's house, and without a word, they removed the bucket with the head and left. Melanie then spent the next three weeks contemplating if she should call the police.

———

Police thought Melanie's story was difficult to believe but decided to do a little research to try and verify it. The first step was to search police databases for the names of Mihaly Illes, Derrick Madinsky, and Javan Dowling.

A quick search through police computers confirmed that Mihaly Illes was a well-known criminal. They found his prior arrests, deportation, and known drug dealing associates, one of whom was Derrick Madinsky.

Javan Dowling had a police record as well. In addition to several drug-related arrests, Javan Dowling had been reported missing by family members right around the time that Melanie claimed to have seen his head in the bucket. Detectives were beginning to realize that Melanie's story could actually be true.

Luckily for detectives, it wasn't hard to track down Mihaly Illes. He was already in police custody, waiting to be deported back to Hungary again. Before speaking to Illes, however, they wanted to talk to Derrick Madinsky. Madinsky was also well-known to police and had his fair share of drug-related arrests. Yet, when police approached him for questioning, he said nothing. He acknowledged he was friends with Mihaly Illes but said nothing of a murder or a head in a bucket.

Detectives then looked into Melanie's story of the van. She had told police that she had seen Madinsky cleaning the inside of a van. Vehicle records showed that Madinsky had recently sold a van, and police recovered it from a used car sales lot.

A thorough forensic analysis was performed on the inside of the van. In addition to photographs and fingerprint analysis, police used a hema stick to search for the presence of blood. A hema stick is a small stick coated with a blood-sensitive chemical. It indicates the presence of blood when touched to a surface and then sprayed with distilled water. The analysis of the van came back positive for human blood, but police needed to find out if the blood belonged to Javan Dowling.

All three of the drug dealers were avid bodybuilders, and when investigators searched Javan Dowling's home, they found a weight-lifting glove. Inside the glove, police recovered skin cells that matched the DNA from the blood found in the van. There was now no question in the detectives' minds that Melanie's story was credible. They had proof that Dowling had bled in the van, but they didn't have definitive proof that he was dead.

Detectives knew that Derrick Madinsky was involved in the crime, so they got a warrant to wiretap his cell phone. After listening to his phone calls, they realized that Madinsky was still helping Illes run the drug operation from prison. Investigators then assigned an undercover police officer to infiltrate the drug ring. Still, nobody was saying a word about Javan Dowling or a murder.

Unable to get the evidence they needed, the police asked for the help of Melanie Ovalle. Detectives had also wiretapped the phone of Illes' girlfriend, Lee-Ann Price. Reluctantly, Melanie agreed to call Lee-Ann and try to get her to talk about the murder.

Melanie called Lee-Ann's tapped phone and expressed her concern about seeing the head in the bucket. She told Lee-Ann that she was riddled with guilt and considering going to the police with the information. Without admitting anything over the phone, Lee-Ann quickly tried to settle her down and told her that she would call her back. Immediately after hanging up with Melanie, Lee-Ann called Mihaly Illes at the prison.

When Lee-Ann called the prison, the police thought she would speak to Illes about the murder. However, they were shocked to hear her say nothing about her conversation with Melanie or the murder. Instead, she told Illes that the two of them needed to get married. Illes was confused, but she assured him she would explain it later. Detectives realized that Lee-Ann knew precisely what she was doing. She knew that if they were married, she couldn't be compelled to testify against her husband. Two days later, Lee-Ann and Mihaly Illes were married in the prison chapel.

Illes was due to be deported from Canada soon. Detectives needed to quickly come up with evidence that a murder had occurred before he was deported, or they may have lost their chance at a conviction. Melanie was also worried about his release. She knew that Illes was able to run his business from prison; he could easily have her killed. She also knew that he had been deported in the past, but that hadn't stopped him from coming back to the country.

With only ten days left before Illes was due to be deported, he was charged with first-degree murder despite no evidence of a body. The charge gave them some leverage to put on Derrick Madinsky. They gave Madinsky a choice: participate in the prosecution of his friend, Illes, or be charged as an accomplice in the murder of Javan Dowling.

Madinsky was a career criminal and surprisingly unfazed after more than ten hours of questioning. Detectives then offered him complete immunity if he testified against Illes. He accepted the offer and agreed to tell the whole story of what happened to Javan Dowling.

———

Madinsky told police that he, Illes, and Dowling were planning on going to a movie together. Illes was in the van's back seat while Madinsky drove, and Dowling was in the passenger seat. As they drove through West Vancouver, Illes asked Dowling to reach over on the dashboard and turn off the van's interior light. As Dowling leaned over the middle of the van, Illes pulled out his revolver and shot Dowling four times in the back of the head. After the shots, Illes mumbled,

"There's not enough room for fags in this world."

Illes then reclined the passenger seat all the way back so the body couldn't be seen from the street, and they drove back to their garage, then parked the van inside.

Once inside the garage, they dragged the body out. Illes instructed Madinsky to clean the inside of the van. Madinsky claimed that Illes took Dowling's body into another room and severed his head.

Illes told Madinsky that, because of Dowling's drug addiction, he shorted a particularly important client. That client threatened Illes, telling him they would seek retribution if he didn't take care of the guy that shorted them. Illes took that to mean they would kill him. He told Madinsky that he severed his head to prove to the client that he'd taken care of the problem employee.

Madinsky told police that he didn't see the body or head of Dowling until a week later when Illes asked for help getting rid of it. Illes had planned to bury the body in the woods and cover it with lime. Illes was under the assumption that lime helped a body decompose more rapidly. Madinsky and Illes then drove forty miles north to a remote wooded area near Squamish, B.C., to bury the body.

————

The judge in Vancouver told detectives that they had one day to present evidence that Illes had murdered Dowling. Without a body, they would have to deport him back to Hungary.

Police then had Madinsky take them to where they buried the body. In a shallow grave, they found the head of Javan Dowling. The head was well-preserved – Illes had been watching too many mobster movies and had mistakenly covered the head with lime rather than lye. Lye would have sped up the decomposition, but lime actually acted as a preservative. Just as Madinsky had told them, Javan Dowling had four bullet wounds in the back of his head.

During the trial, they turned on each other. Madinsky testified against Illes, and Illes claimed that Madinsky was the one that killed Dowling. In March 2003, a British Columbia Supreme Court jury found Mihaly Illes guilty of first-degree murder. He was sentenced to life in prison without the chance of parole for twenty-five years.

————

Seven years later, the defense claimed that the judge had made a mistake when instructing the jury and that Illes' rights had been violated. The defense also argued that the prosecution had not disclosed specific evidence. As a result, Illes had his verdict overturned and was awarded a second trial.

During the second trial, the defense argued that letters written to Lee-Ann and other friends of Mihaly Illes were not presented as evidence. They insisted that those letters proved his innocence.

The letters, however, were filled with elaborate conspiracy theories in which he blamed Derrick Madinsky and Melanie Ovalle for the murders. He claimed Melanie's description of events was motivated by jealousy because her friend, Lee-Ann, was spending all her time with him. He also suspected that Javan Dowling was still alive and in hiding. Another letter claimed that he believed the blood found in the van was from when Javan and his boyfriend got in a fistfight, and he got a bloody nose. Yet another letter claimed that there was no murder at all, and the police were fabricating evidence and playing "KGB mind tricks."

Using yet another letter, the prosecution proved that the prior letters were all written as a ruse, specifically for the intention of the police intercepting them. The letter that the prosecution presented read:

> "There is our defense. The [white] letter says it all. Who killed whom, and why... It will be like an ACE in our pock-et. This could decide the case. Make it, or brake [sic] it."

After the second trial, Illes was again found guilty and sentenced to life in prison with no parole for twenty-five years.

Coincidentally, just three months after Javan Dowling's death, Derrick Madinsky was involved in another drug-related murder in California.

Madinsky and his associate, Garry Favell, traveled to Los Angeles for another of their marijuana for crack cocaine deals. This time they brought a new guy with them, Joe Bralic. Bralic was not a career criminal like Favell and Madinsky but was headed in that direction. He'd heard that he could make some quick cash by handling the transaction, and they arranged for him to meet with the Los Angeles buyers.

The three men traveled to Los Angeles together, but Madinsky and Favell were the only ones to return to Canada. On July 5, 2002, Joe Bralic's body was discovered behind a Discount Tire store in Fullerton, California. He had been shot, and his body was wrapped in plastic, found lying between two parked cars. Joe Bralic's killer has never been found.

CHAPTER 8
ARIZONA TORSO
MURDER #1

In 1993, forty-one-year-old Valerie Pape was living in New York City and working odd jobs, with almost no assets to speak of. Living on a shoestring, she rented a car and stayed with friends. She had immigrated from France and cared for an elderly man named Howard Pomerantz when she met his son, Ira Pomerantz.

Ira was a loud, brash, fifty-four-year-old New Yorker. Quite the opposite of Valerie. She was a petite blonde, stood at five-foot-two, and only weighed one hundred and ten pounds. Her friends described her as sweet, gentle, kind, sensitive, and always meticulously dressed. Despite her lack of income, she was obsessed with fashion and wouldn't leave the house without her hair and makeup perfect and dressed smartly.

Valerie Pape & Ira Pomerantz

Despite their thirteen-year age difference, Ira and Valerie hit it off, and within two years they were married. At their wedding on November 18, 1995, Valerie wore a dress from Neiman Marcus, and her close friend from France, Michel Sauvage, gave her away.

That same year, they moved to the posh McCormick Ranch neighborhood in North Scottsdale, Arizona. Valerie enjoyed the year-round warm weather, and the couple quickly became well-known socialites in the area. Valerie was very fit, jogged through the affluent neighborhood daily, and regularly hiked Scottsdale's Camelback Mountain.

Ira Pomerantz opened two bars in nearby Chandler, Arizona, while Valerie attended the Allure Career College of Beauty in Scottsdale. Then in 1997, with the financial help of Ira, Valerie opened her own hair salon and art gallery, the Valerie Pape Beauty Gallery, in the upscale Old Town area of Scottsdale.

Valerie's friend, Michel Sauvage, had followed the couple to Scottsdale and worked at the salon, answering phones and taking reservations. To keep his immigration status and stay in the country, Valerie listed Michel as one of the officers of her company.

Ira Pomerantz was known as a good, friendly man, but he had a drinking problem and a temper. In 1998, he was arrested for DUI. He was also known for not being a very good businessman. He became notorious for refusing to pay his employees, overcharging his customers, watering down drinks, and not obeying liquor laws. Eventually, he was fined by the liquor control board for serving drinks to underage customers and serving drinks after hours.

With stacking debt and business going badly, Ira lost the lease on one of his bars. The closing of the second bar wasn't far behind, and in 1999, he was in the process of filing for bankruptcy.

It didn't help his financial matters that Valerie had grown accustomed to spending their money on her lavish lifestyle. She drove a brand new Jaguar and dressed in only the finest clothes. As a result, the couple constantly argued over their dwindling money supply, and Ira had difficulty controlling his temper.

Michel Sauvage was very close with the couple, and by early 1999, he had moved into Ira and Valerie's 2,900-square-foot home. Michel was a constant third figure in the relationship, rarely leaving Valerie's side. On top of the money problems, Ira became very suspicious that Valerie and Michel were having an affair.

Ira told his friends that he couldn't keep up with Valerie's lavish spending, and she was bleeding him dry. He said he was planning to divorce her.

The arguments between Ira and Valerie got so bad that she took self-defense lessons and learned how to shoot a handgun. Ira had an extensive collection of handguns, and she claimed she was worried he would use one on her.

In September 1999, Valerie needed to get away from Ira, so she and Michel temporarily moved in with her friend, Merle Bianchi. Unfortunately, Merle was having some problems of her own. While Valerie and Michel were staying at her home, Merle reported her husband missing. Valerie and Ira reconciled not long afterward, and they moved back in with Ira.

It was just a week after Valerie and Michel moved out that Merle's husband, Ron Bianchi, was found in the forest eighty miles north of Scottsdale in Payson, Arizona. He was dead.

Once back home, the conflicts between Valerie and Ira continued. During one of their heated arguments in October 1999, Valerie accused him of running into the kitchen, opening a drawer, and throwing kitchen knives at her. Ira denied the allegation, but Valerie was given a court order of protection against him and he was ordered to move out of his own home.

Within a few days, he had violated the court order. She called the police, but a week later they had reconciled. Ira moved back into the house again. She told the court,

> "I have received apologies and want to give him another chance."

Police were called to the couple's house at least six times during the late nineties for assorted reasons, ranging from burglary to aggravated assault and violation of a protective order.

In the early morning hours of January 28, 2000, twenty-five miles away from Scottsdale in East Mesa, a truck driver was dropping off his 5:00 a.m. delivery behind Basha's grocery store on Power Road and McDowell Road. At that time of the morning, he thought it was odd to see a blue Jaguar pull up next to the dumpsters behind the store. He watched as a petite blonde woman wearing high heels, gloves, sunglasses, and a jumpsuit opened her trunk and took out a large object wrapped in plastic. The tiny woman struggled to lift the package over her head and into the dumpster. The delivery driver took down the Jaguar's license plate and watched as the woman drove away.

After the car was gone, the man walked over to the dumpster to peek inside and found what appeared to be a large body part wrapped in plastic sheeting. He immediately called the police.

When police arrived, they recovered the torso of a male body missing its arms, legs, and head. When investigators ran the license plate number of the Jaguar, it came back registered to Valerie Pape.

Police announced the details of the finding,

> "The head had been severed at the base of the neck, both arms cut off at the shoulders, the lower half of the body dismembered at the waist."

When police arrested Valerie Pape at her hair salon, her co-workers and friends were stunned. There was no way the petite, sweet woman could have been the one that dumped a human torso, let alone dismembered it.

One of Valerie's close friends was Republican Arizona Senator Russell Bowers. His personal assistant was Valerie's friend, Merle Bianchi, whose husband had also been murdered. Bowers was shocked at the news of Pape's arrest and professed her innocence to reporters,

"Valerie Pape showed my paintings in her salon. She's a very gentle, decent person, and I'm astonished at this. I think highly of Valerie, and it makes me sick to my stomach to think this could happen to her. I knew her husband beat her up. I've seen her face. It was a sickening thing."

———

During her interrogation on January 28, Valerie Pape admitted that she dumped Ira's body in the dumpster behind the supermarket but claimed she didn't kill him.

She explained that she came home from work to find Ira dead, face up, and in a pool of blood on the floor. There was a bullet hole in his back and a gun on the floor nearby. She said she only dumped the body in the dumpster to avoid being accused of his murder.

However, she refused to admit to dismembering the body or say where the remaining parts of her husband's body were. She also said that she had found the body on January 24, four days prior, but refused to say what she did with the body during those four days.

Valerie Pape was arrested and charged with first-degree murder. Investigators searched the couple's house and Valerie's 1997 Jaguar. Beneath the back seat of the Jaguar, they found the handgun that was used to shoot Ira in the back.

Police also searched the home of Valerie's friend, Merle Bianchi. They found it all too coincidental that the husband of Valerie's close friend was murdered just four months prior. The ballistics team analyzed the handgun found in Valerie's car against the bullets that killed Ronald Bianchi, but it wasn't a match.

Dismembering and disposing of a body would be a difficult task, particularly for a woman who was only five-foot-two and 110 pounds. Detectives thought she might have had some help, but Valerie didn't say a word.

After searching their home, investigators found the receipt for an electric reciprocating saw and saw blades that Valerie had purchased from a local department store a few weeks before the murder. That, coupled with the fact that she had taken shooting lessons in the prior months, showed that the murder was intentional and premeditated.

Police then searched the Chandler bar that Ira had recently closed. They believed she might have transported the body to the bar and frozen it in the walk-in freezer. A frozen body would have made dismembering the body much more manageable and delayed the decomposition. But, again, there was no way she could have done it alone. She had to have had help.

Valerie Pape was held without bail. Because she was a French citizen, she was placed on an immigration hold – meaning that if she were released for any reason, she would be turned over to the Immigration and Naturalization Service.

Despite their efforts, police found no evidence of Valerie having had help to kill Ira and they never discovered his remaining body parts. There was overwhelming suspicion that Michel Sauvage had a hand in the murder, but a lack of evidence prevented police from bringing any charges against him.

Unfortunately for prosecutors, no blood evidence was linked to Pape, and the bullet that killed him was never recovered. It was believed that the bullet entered the back of his neck and was still in his head, which, again, was never recovered. The saw and blades were also never found.

Additionally, prosecutors were concerned that the claims of domestic abuse might persuade a jury that the murder wasn't premeditated, and she may have been acquitted of a first-degree murder charge. Thus, rather than risk a not-guilty verdict, they offered her a plea deal.

———

After two and a half years in jail awaiting trial, as part of the plea deal, Valerie Pape admitted she shot Ira Pomerantz during an argument. She pleaded guilty to a lesser charge of second-degree murder with a prison sentence of just sixteen years.

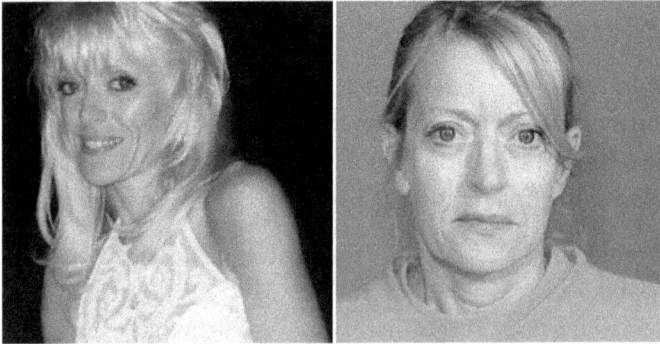

Valerie Pape

During her time in prison, she served as the prison's beautician and cut the hair of other inmates and prison employees.

In 2006, a Department of Corrections director approved a transfer for Pape to finish her prison sentence in France. She was flown to Oklahoma City in preparation for the move, but Ira Pomerantz's daughters pressured the Department of Corrections to reverse the move. They were concerned because, after her arrival back in France, the country was under no obligation to have Pape finish her sentence. Valerie Pape was then returned to Arizona to finish her sentence.

After serving her sentence, at sixty-three years old, Valerie Pape was released from prison in 2016 and deported back to her native France.

CHAPTER 9
ARIZONA TORSO MURDER #2

The story of Marjorie Orbin is eerily similar to the Valerie Pape story. It occurred just four years and seven months after the Valerie Pape murder in the same city of Scottsdale, Arizona. The body was found in a similar condition – a dismembered torso – and both killers were trophy wives of wealthy men. It makes you wonder if she was mimicking the Valerie Pape case.

———

Marjorie Orbin led a somewhat extraordinary life. But to hear her say it, calling her just a stripper would be unfairly downplaying her career. Yes, she did some stripping, but in her mind she was also a talented dancer, a showgirl, and a choreographer.

She officially began her dancing career when she was just eighteen in Orlando, Florida, where she danced at a downtown tourist attraction called Church Street Station. She performed line dances, jazz, and clogging routines. Marjorie was extremely ambitious, and within a year she had choreo-graphed the routines and been promoted to manager of another location called Cheyenne Station.

She had always dreamed of being a mother, but at just eigh-teen, she was diagnosed with endometriosis – a painful disorder that affects the lining of the uterus. Though preg-nancy is possible with endometriosis patients, it's unlikely; she was told that she could not have children. This news was a severe disappointment to Marjorie. In that moment, she decided that since she couldn't lead a life for her children, she would live her life solely for herself and her career.

> "I could walk out of any situation. That may sound cold and
> callous, but the only person I needed to worry about
> was me."

Relationships came one after another and Marjorie found herself hopping from man to man. By the time she was thirty-five years old, she had been married and divorced six times. Most of the time, she had already found another lover before divorcing her previous husband.

Marjorie Orbin

In 1985, before the ink was dry on her second divorce, Marjorie found herself living with a hairdresser named Luke. Luke came from a wealthy family that offered him a condo if he moved back home to Cincinnati. Marjorie quit her job and followed Luke. As they drove across the country, Luke received word that the condo wouldn't be ready for another month, so he suggested they go to Las Vegas temporarily. He had friends there who owned a hair salon that he could work in for a few weeks until the Cincinnati condo was ready for them.

Luke ended up gambling away their $8,000 savings, and the salon job was non-existent. Marjorie packed her car and left, intending to drive back to Florida, but her car didn't last that long. As she drove through Phoenix, Arizona, her car broke down: it needed an expensive part that would take ten days to fix.

Marjorie was wondering how she would pay for the repair work when she noticed a strip club called Bourbon Street Circus and applied for a job. At that point, she had never done any stripping, but it seemed to come naturally to her. Since she was classically trained in dance, she quickly realized she could work the pole better than any of the other girls.

Marjorie was statuesque and beautiful, with platinum blonde hair, long legs, and a flawless body. Within days, she was easily the most popular dancer in the club. The patrons were infatuated with her, and she was pulling in $500-$600 per night. One of those patrons was twenty-six-year-old Jay Orbin.

Jay was a regular at Bourbon Street Circus and almost every other strip club in the Phoenix area. He was well-known by strippers and club management as one of the best customers.

But Jay was on the chubby side and didn't have the greatest fashion sense. Known for his balding-yet-thick, curly, black hair, plus rosy cheeks, cowboy boots, and a diamond pinkie ring, he came across as looking much like a used car salesman. According to his friends, however, Jay was funny, charming, and had a heart of gold.

Jay had his own business, Jayhawk International, selling Native American items like turquoise jewelry, kachina dolls, maps, and bows and arrows. His work was profitable and took him all over the country on sales calls. He traveled three out of four weeks per month and spent his free time in strip clubs all over the country.

Jay had dated many strippers throughout the years, but he was utterly captivated by Marjorie. He came in to see her dance and buy her drinks every chance he got. Though he asked to see her outside the club, she refused. Still, he persisted. After about two months, she agreed to go on an afternoon date with him.

Despite his persistence, she still didn't see herself attracted to him. He was very nice but not exactly her type. Eventually, he paid for her car to get fixed and offered to let her move into his home. Marjorie had been living in a hotel, and he offered to let her stay in a spare room at his house for free. He was gone traveling the country most of the time anyway. She agreed and moved in.

Jay & Marjorie Orbin

Though Jay tried to get her to be romantic with him, at one point even proposing marriage, Marjorie wanted more from her life and eventually moved back to Florida. Through the years, the two of them lost contact.

———

While back in Florida, Marjorie dated Michael J. Peter. Michael was well-known the world over for transforming the strip club industry. He took the industry from taboo to mainstream. He bought strip clubs all over the world and made billions. For a short time, he and Marjorie were engaged.

Marjorie traveled the world with him, and he gave her a role in his low-budget (unwatchable) movie *No More Dirty Deals*, as well as got her a small spot in Motley Crue's *"Girls Girls Girls"* video. The song became an anthem at strip clubs around the world. Marjorie became the "choreographer" in his clubs, although the strip clubs didn't have much in the way of choreography. Like all of Marjorie's relationships, it didn't last forever. The two stayed on good terms, but Marjorie eventually made her way back to Las Vegas.

———

Years later, in 1993, Jay was on a business trip driving through Las Vegas when he noticed a billboard for an adult revue at one of the big casinos. He instantly recognized Marjorie in the advertisement and bought tickets for the show that night.

In the years that passed, Marjorie had become a Vegas show-girl and choreographer for adult revue shows. The two met that night, and Jay realized that he still felt the same way he did years before.

Both Marjorie and Jay were making good money by now, but Marjorie still wanted more than anything to have a family. Realizing this, Jay proposed marriage again – but this time, he had a plan. He told her that she could move in with him in Scottsdale, Arizona, quit stripping, and he would pay for fertility treatments until she got pregnant.

Marjorie liked this idea; in 1994, Jay and Marjorie married at the Little White Wedding Chapel in Las Vegas. This was the same little chapel where celebrities like Frank Sinatra, Judy Garland, Bruce Willis, and Britney Spears were married.

Despite her diagnosis, the fertility treatment worked, and they had a son named Noah in August 1996. Although their relationship was doing well, Marjorie had sizable debt and problems paying the Internal Revenue Service. So, to protect Jay's business assets from being seized by the IRS, they divorced while still remaining together.

For almost ten years, Marjorie Orbin lived the life of a typical suburban housewife, raising her son while Jay traveled the country on sales calls. Although the relationship had lasted much longer than her previous six marriages, she became bored like she had with the others and started seeking other men.

Her infidelities started in 2004. Her first affair was with her son's eighteen-year-old karate instructor. The second was with a sixty-year-old bodybuilder, Larry Weisberg, who she met at her gym. With Jay on the road for three weeks every month, it was easy for Marjorie to hide her affairs from Jay. While Jay was gone, Larry lived at the house with Marjorie full-time.

August 28, 2004, was Noah's eighth birthday. After the birthday party, Jay headed back out on the road. This time, he was on his way to Florida for three weeks. However, once Jay got halfway to Florida, Hurricane Francis had grown too large, and he turned around to return home. With this change, he could make it back to Scottsdale to be home by his own birthday, September 8.

On the afternoon of September 8, as he was driving into the Phoenix area, Jay called his parents, as he did several times a week. He told his mother that his trip had been cut short, and he was almost back home, just in time for his forty-fifth birthday. As he pulled into his neighborhood, he told his mother he would call her back later in the day. She never got that call.

———

Over the next week, when friends and family hadn't heard from Jay on his birthday, they got worried and called

Marjorie. Marjorie wasn't worried at all; she said that Jay hadn't come home. She said he'd called and said he had to go on another sales trip and wouldn't be home until September 22. She told them she hadn't seen him since their son's birthday on August 28.

In the weeks that followed, Jay's family and friends were getting more and more worried, but Marjorie showed no concern. On September 20, several of Jay's friends received calls from Jay's cell phone. However, when they answered, there was no one on the other end.

When September 22 rolled around, Jay still hadn't come home or even called, so they pressured her to finally call the police and report him missing. Reluctantly, she called.

Although Marjorie had reported Jay as missing, she was frequently unavailable to discuss the matter with the police. Police needed the license plate number of Jay's Ford Bronco to use plate recognition to search for it, but by September 28, detectives had left three messages for Marjorie. She hadn't returned their calls. When Detective Jan Butcher of the Missing Persons Unit finally got Marjorie on the phone, she was combative:

> Butcher: "I kind of get the feeling that you're really not available and willing to help us out trying to locate…."

> Marjorie: "I speak more matter of factly; that doesn't mean that I do not care. Just because I'm not running around crying and in hysteria doesn't mean that I'm not concerned and not doing anything."

Her reluctance to help and defensive posturing made investigators suspicious of her from the very beginning.

When police checked Jay's bank accounts and credit cards, they realized large amounts of money were being pulled out of his accounts. The signatures on the receipts were Jay Orbin's, but they quickly realized that he hadn't actually signed them – Marjorie had. Within days of Jay's disappearance, Marjorie had pulled out the maximum amount from ATMs each day. When detectives asked about the withdrawals, Marjorie explained she needed the cash to pay the bills. But when investigators noticed that she had bought a baby grand piano for almost $12,000 with the money, it raised even more red flags.

Beginning on September 9, the day after Jay went missing, Marjorie pulled out over $100,000 from Jay's personal bank accounts and over $45,000 from his business account. She was also selling merchandise from Jay's business.

When investigators discovered that Jay had a $1 million life insurance policy with Marjorie as the beneficiary, they knew the situation was going to end badly.

Detective Butcher called Marjorie again to ask her to come in to take a polygraph test, but her tone became combative,

> Det. Butcher: "Can we schedule to take a polygraph tomorrow?"
>
> Marjorie: "She wants me to take a polygraph tomorrow!" (Speaking to someone else in the room.)
>
> Larry: "You tell her to go fuck herself!"
>
> Det. Butcher: "Who was that?"
>
> Marjorie: "None of your fucking business! It's a friend of mine. Is this conversation being recorded?"
>
> Det. Butcher: "Yes, it is."

Marjorie: "It is. Ok. I would like a copy of that."

After phone negotiations proved to be unproductive, Scottsdale police obtained a search warrant for Jay Orbin's house. When the SWAT team broke down the door to the Orbin home, they were attacked by a well-built man. That man was Larry Weisberg, Marjorie's bodybuilder boyfriend. When Larry attacked the SWAT team, they quickly tased and hit him in the face, breaking his nose.

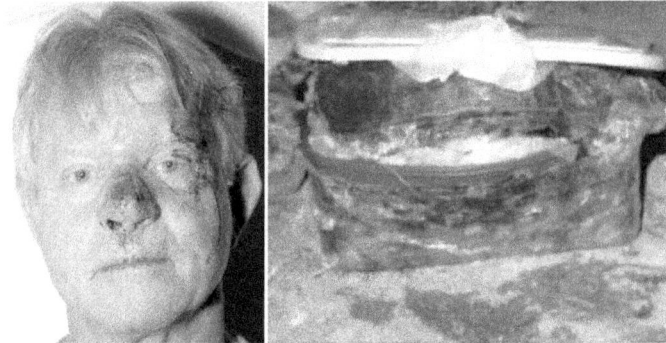

Larry Weisberg & The Rubbermaid Container

Once inside the house, they found business credit cards and checkbooks that Jay Orbin typically used on his business trips. Detective Butcher now believed that this was not just a missing person investigation. Everything she knew pointed to it being a homicide.

———

On October 23, on the corner of Tatum Road and Dynamite Road, a transient was roaming around a piece of Arizona state trust land in the desert, just fifty feet from the road. Though it was desert, it wasn't remote. The roads were busy, and housing developments were only a few hundred feet away.

The man came across a large object wrapped in black plastic garbage bags and sealed with tape. He pulled the tape off and ripped the black plastic. Inside he found a large, blue Rubbermaid storage container. When he opened the lid of the container, he stumbled back in shock. Aside from the horrible stench, he was shocked to see a belt buckle – and what appeared to be the hairy belly of a man. He immediately ran to a nearby store and called the police.

When police arrived, they discovered it wasn't a whole body but only a half-torso. The male body had been cut just below the ribcage, and the legs had been severed at the knees. The internal organs of the lower half of the torso had been removed. The body had been dismembered while clothed, still wearing jean shorts and a brown leather belt.

At the bottom of the container was a .38 caliber bullet, mixed currency totaling $459.10, and a keyring with eleven keys. The Rubbermaid container was new and still had the UPC sticker on the bottom.

During the autopsy, the medical examiner determined that the body had been previously frozen for an extended period before it was dismembered. From the markings on the bones, they could tell that the body had been dismembered with a saw of some sort.

———

Six weeks after Jay Orbin went missing, they now believed that they had found his remains just a few miles from his home. DNA tests later confirmed their suspicions. They also believed that Marjorie Orbin had placed the torso there because she wanted the body to be found. After all, in order for her to collect the $1 million insurance claim, Jay had to be confirmed dead. She couldn't collect if he was just missing.

Two days after the torso was found, Jay Orbin's green Ford Bronco was found parked in a residential neighborhood just a few blocks from their home. Detectives took the keys that were found in the bottom of the Rubbermaid container, and as they suspected, they opened and started the Bronco. The remaining keys opened the Orbin home and Jay's office. Three witnesses from the neighborhood told police they saw a woman matching Marjorie's description near the Bronco sometime around September 8.

Three weeks after Jay's body was found, police brought Marjorie in for questioning – not for Jay's murder but for forging his signature when she bought computers at a Circuit City electronics store. However, Marjorie explained that she had been signing his name for years and didn't realize there was anything wrong with using his credit cards after his death.

The more investigating detectives did, the more evidence started to pile up. When searching the Orbin home, investigators found a receipt from Lowe's hardware store dated two days after Jay went missing. On the receipt for that purchase was a slew of mops, various cleaning products, black plastic bags, and two fifty-gallon blue Rubbermaid containers. They were precisely the same type as the container in which Jay's disemboweled torso had been found. In fact, the UPC code on the container they found matched the code from the receipt. Still, the most crucial piece of evidence was a videotape they acquired from that Lowes store dated September 10. The tape showed Marjorie at the checkout counter, purchasing the murder clean-up supplies – and it clearly showed her purchasing the large blue containers.

In Jay's office, investigators found an open package of jigsaw blades missing two blades. The medical examiner determined that the cutting pattern on his bones was consistent with that type of blade.

Back at the Orbin home, they discovered that the garage floor had recently been acid-washed, and a thick layer of decorative epoxy had been installed over the cement, eliminating any chance of finding trace forensic evidence.

On December 6, 2004, Marjorie Orbin was arrested at her home and charged with first-degree murder, fraud, and theft. She was held without bail, and their son, Noah, was sent to live with Jay's parents.

Initially, Larry Weisberg was also a suspect. A search of his home and vehicle showed that he had access to the Orbin home. He had a garage door opener for their garage in his vehicle, so he had the means, but there was no hard evidence against him. All of the evidence pointed directly at Marjorie. With a first-degree murder charge in the state of Arizona, she now faced the possibility of the death penalty.

In a controversial move, the prosecution gave Larry Weisberg complete immunity in the case if he testified against Marjorie.

Faced with the overwhelming evidence against her, Marjorie's attorneys advised her to take a plea deal of a lesser charge to avoid the death penalty, but she refused,

> "I will never let my son hear me say that I did this to his father. I'll let them kill me first."

———

Marjorie spent the next four years behind bars awaiting trial. During the trial, the defense tried to argue that Jay Orbin weighed at least 250 pounds, and it would have been too physically demanding for Marjorie to dismember and move a body that large. But Marjorie wasn't exactly petite: she was a tall, muscular woman that worked out religiously.

The defense also tried to persuade the jury that Larry Weisberg was responsible for Jay's death, but they offered no evidence. They argued that he was aggressive enough to confront a SWAT team, and as a bodybuilder, he was certainly strong enough to dispose of a body.

The prosecutors countered that defense by saying Larry Weisberg was just another in Marjorie's long list of infidelities. They also pointed out that investigators found no evidence that Larry was involved in the murder at all.

The prosecution also brought in the nineteen-year-old karate instructor that she was sleeping with and her former friends, who claimed she often talked badly of Jay. The karate instructor and Larry Weisberg both claimed that Marjorie was skilled in the art of seduction.

The prosecution also called her cellmate from prison, Sophia Johnson, to the stand. Sophia testified that Marjorie had often complained to her that Jay was fat and disgusting. Sophia claimed that Marjorie confessed to her that she shot Jay, froze his body, thawed the corpse, and then cut off his arms, legs, and head.

The only witness called by the defense was a character witness, Marjorie's former billionaire lover, Michael J. Peter.

Peter painted a glowing picture of Marjorie as a good, loving mother, but it wasn't enough to sway the jury.

The trial lasted eight months, but it took only seven hours for the jury to come back with a guilty verdict.

As Judge Arthur Anderson handed down the sentence to Marjorie, he compared her case to yet another Arizona killer: Winnie Ruth Judd, who murdered and dismembered her two friends in 1931 and stuffed their remains into steamer trunks.

At the sentencing on October 1, 2009, Marjorie had her son to thank for avoiding the death penalty. The jury chose to sentence her to life in prison without the chance of parole rather than death.

> "We all decided that the son is the innocent victim here. We all walked out of there feeling good." - Juror, Stan Brown

> "This is what we wanted all along. From the beginning, we didn't want to kill the boy's mother, and we wanted life." - Jay Orbin's brother, Jake Orbin

———

To this day, Marjorie Orbin claims that Larry Weisberg shot Jay Orbin in the garage of their home, she never saw Jay's dead body, and she certainly didn't dismember or dispose of the corpse. Marjorie admitted that she helped cover up the murder but insisted she didn't kill him.

She claimed to TV crews of the show *48 Hours* that Weisberg was a very violent man and shot Jay in their garage. She said that Larry threatened to kill her son if she told the police he did it. She claimed that Weisberg said,

"It's just that easy to snap that kid's scrawny neck if you don't do what you're told."

Although she claimed that Weisberg threatened her when in front of TV crews, she never told this story to the police.

———

Currently, Marjorie's profile on writeaprisoner.com reads:

Growing up in Miami, Florida, the sunshine and water were a big part of my life, playing on the beaches, diving, surfing, sailing, playing beach volleyball.

The little girl in ballet class was the start of a lifelong love of dance. I had quite a career as a professional dancer and choreographer, from Disney World to cruise ships in Las Vegas shows. Paris, Japan, Germany. Even dancing on Rock videos. Motley Crew "Girl, Girls, Girls." Traveling all over the world. I had many exciting adventures.

Then... one unforeseen incident changed everything. But even now, I do my best to be positive and create a meaningful life for myself.

I am strong and healthy and active. I teach aerobics classes. I am tall, slender and have long blonde hair. I have a pretty silly sense of humor sometimes. I read, watch trashy TV and stay out of drama.

I miss traveling, good food, the ocean, interesting friends and romance. I would love to meet new friends from the real world that might share their adventures or maybe just talk.

Please write to me directly.

Marjorie

CHAPTER 10
THE TACOMA MURDERS

When the use of DNA as a crime-solving tool was first introduced in 1986, it was used to convict criminals who left samples of their DNA at a crime scene. Unfortunately, it took a long time to process and was extremely costly.

As time went by and technology improved, it became less costly and took less time to test, but there was still the matter of finding a match. Investigators needed to have a suspect and acquire that suspect's DNA before they could find a match.

Then, in the 1990s, CODIS (Combined DNA Index System) was introduced. The FBI established CODIS as a central database of known DNA samples. This was a considerable advancement: if investigators didn't have a suspect, they could check in CODIS to find a possible match. The only problem was that the person in question had to have been convicted of a crime in the past *and* to have had their DNA taken at that time. Currently, DNA laws vary per state in the United States. Some states take DNA for felony arrests, some for misdemeanors; some apply to juveniles, some don't. However, as of 2019, most states will take DNA for felony arrests.

In the past few years, another huge advancement in DNA crime-fighting has happened. Now, people freely give their DNA in search of their ancestral roots. Sites like 23andme.com (co-founded by Ann Wojcicki, wife of Google's Sergey Brin), GedMatch.com, and Ancestry.com have acquired vast amounts of the general public's DNA, meaning the DNA of people who have not necessarily committed any crimes. With that DNA comes a world of new possibilities. This method was used in 2018 in the high-profile case of the Golden State Killer.

The disappearance of Michella Welch also used this new process. Her case was thought to be linked to a similar murder that happened the same year, but DNA eventually proved there were two separate killers. These two cases are prime examples of the unsettling fact that there are monsters that walk among us, undetected.

———

On March 26, during Spring Break of 1986, twelve-year-old Michella Welch and her two younger sisters rode their bicycles to Puget Park in North Tacoma, Washington, at around 10:00 a.m.

After a few hours of playing in the park, the girls were getting hungry and Michella decided to ride her bike back home to prepare some lunch and bring it back for herself and her sisters. When she returned to the park, her sisters weren't around. Michella put the brown paper bag with their lunches on a picnic bench, locked her bike up, and went looking for her sisters.

Around 1:15 p.m., Michella's sisters returned and found her bike and the lunches, but there was no sign of Michella. The two sisters wandered around the park, looking for her and calling her name, but they got no reply. Worried and scared, they went home. By 3:10 p.m., the Tacoma Police had been called, and an official search began.

At 11:27 that evening, the police search and rescue dogs found Michella's body near a fire-pit area in the park. She had been sexually assaulted, suffered blunt force trauma to her head, and her throat had been slit.

A classmate of Michella told investigators that he saw a suspicious-looking man beneath the Proctor Bridge looking at young girls, but the man was never found.

———

In early August of that same year, just five months after Michella was murdered, thirteen-year-old Jennifer Bastian was riding her bicycle in Point Defiance Park. The park was just three miles from the park where Michella had disappeared. Jennifer was practicing for a bike ride she had planned in the San Juan Islands later that summer.

Jennifer took out her new Schwinn eighteen-speed bike, promised her mother she'd be home for dinner by 6:30, and headed for a road called Five Mile Drive.

When Jennifer hadn't returned home by 6:30 that evening, her mother became worried. Two hours later, her terrified parents called the police and reported her missing. Police with sniffer dogs searched the park extensively, but there was no sign of Jennifer.

Three teenage boys that went to school with Jennifer recalled seeing her riding her bike at approximately 4:10 p.m. She was riding her bicycle on Five Mile Drive, as she had told her mother, but they said she didn't seem concerned or in any danger.

The police closed the park for two days and recruited members of the Green River Killer Task Force to help with the search, but they had still found nothing after two days of searching.

Three weeks later, joggers found Jennifer's body in a remote area of the park. Her body had been concealed by brush, and her bicycle was located just a few yards away. Her swimsuit bottoms were pulled down around her ankles, and there was evidence that she had been raped. An autopsy showed that Jennifer died of strangulation.

With both crimes happening in the same vicinity, both girls being similar in age and appearance, and both riding their bicycles in the parks, police assumed it was the work of the same killer.

Thousands of tips were called in of possible suspects seen in the area, and police facial sketches were shown on the nightly news. More than 10,000 hours of police work went into the two investigations, but after all their efforts, no credible leads ever turned up. The killer seemed to have vanished into thin air, and both cases went cold for over thirty years.

Though DNA evidence was found at Michella's scene, DNA forensic science was in its infancy in 1986. Even CODIS was unavailable at that time. Still, police saved the DNA samples, knowing that technology would someday change, and they could eventually catch the killer.

———

Twenty-five years later, in 2011, the Tacoma Police Department launched a new division concentrated on looking at older cold cases. The cold cases of Michella and Jennifer were part of the reason the new division was created. Detectives pored through dozens of binders of files for the two cases and over 2,300 names connected to the cases.

Though there had been no useable DNA collected from Jennifer's crime scene at the time, they had saved the swimsuit bottoms she was wearing. With new technology that wasn't available almost thirty years prior, they could now recover male DNA from the swimsuit.

It wasn't until 2016, when the two DNA samples from Jennifer and Michella's murder scenes were compared to each other, that detectives made a startling discovery. For almost thirty years, police had believed that the same person had killed both Jennifer and Michella, but now they realized there were, in fact, two different killers.

Armed with the new DNA results from Jennifer's crime scene, police had a list of 160 suspects. They now needed DNA samples to compare to the semen found on Jennifer's bathing suit.

———

In May 2018, FBI agents knocked on the door of sixty-year-old Robert Washburn, who had lived near Point Defiance

Park at the time but now lived in Eureka, Illinois. He was on the list of 160 potential suspects. Washburn voluntarily gave a sample of his DNA, which matched the DNA found at Jennifer Bastian's murder scene. He was arrested and brought back to Pierce County, Washington, to stand trial.

Robert Washburn & Jennifer Bastian

Washburn first came up on the Tacoma Police's radar when he called in to give a tip on Michella's murder.

Friends and family that knew him as an older man found it hard to fathom Washburn as a child killer. They knew him as a doting father and full-time caretaker for his disabled daughter. Even Washburn's ex-wife had no idea,

> "I would have divorced him and turned him in. I am happy for that family, for that little girl... We never saw this coming. He was always gentle."

Robert Washburn pleaded guilty to the first-degree murder of Jennifer Bastian and was sentenced to twenty-six years in prison.

In the case of finding Michella's killer, police caught an extremely lucky break using Genetic Genealogy.

Typically, DNA evidence was only relevant if there was a suspect to compare it to. Databases like the FBI's CODIS only had the DNA of prior criminals, but if investigators were looking for someone who had never been convicted of a crime then they were out of luck.

Using the DNA from Michella's crime scene, police entered the DNA into a public online DNA-matching website, GEDmatch.com. After uploading the DNA, they were able to create a family tree. The family tree limited the suspects down to two brothers who lived in North Tacoma in 1986 near Puget Park, where Michella was killed.

Police followed sixty-six-year-old Gary Charles Hartman from his job as a nurse at Western State Hospital to a restaurant in Tacoma, where he had lunch with a co-worker. Detectives sat at a table in the restaurant and had lunch just ten feet away. They watched as Hartman finished his lunch, wiped his mouth with a napkin, and placed it in a paper bag. Hartman then left the bag on the table and left the restaurant.

Detectives gathered the napkin containing his DNA and submitted it to the police lab for testing. The DNA was indeed a match to the DNA left at the scene of Michella's murder, which led police to arrest Hartman.

Gary Hartman & Michella Welch

Like Washburn, Hartman led an otherwise completely normal life, and news of his arrest for such a heinous crime shocked his friends and family. Hartman was a father of two who collected vintage cars. He worked as a community nurse specialist at Western State Hospital and had no prior criminal record. Acquaintances described him as a pleasant, even-tempered guy. Hartman had lived within a mile of Puget Park at the time of Michella's murder.

In March 2022, Gary Hartman was convicted and sentenced to twenty-six years in prison.

CHAPTER 11
THE KILLER BRIDE

Kalispell, Montana, is known as the gateway to Glacier National Park. With a population of only 23,000, it was hurled into the national spotlight during the summer of 2013 as the spot of one of the most absurd murders of the year.

Jordan Graham was a shy, introverted, and deeply religious twenty-year-old when she met twenty-three-year-old Cody Johnson. Cody was quite the opposite. He was very outgoing and social, and although they met at a church picnic, he didn't really have an interest in attending church. He was more interested in fast cars and shooting guns than going to church.

Cody was instantly smitten with Jordan, and the two began dating. Although Cody quickly fell madly in love with Jordan, she didn't feel the same way and was unaffectionate. Because of her religion, Jordan didn't believe in sex before marriage – but her lack of affection went beyond just the absence of sex. Their friends noted that the couple never even held hands or flirted together.

But that didn't deter Cody. He tried hard to win over Jordan's love. When they first started dating, Cody told his mother that she was *the one.* He told her that he intended to make Jordan his wife.

Church was very important to Jordan, and one of the first things she insisted Cody do was go to church with her every Sunday. If they were going to have any relationship at all, he would need to be a good Christian like her.

They had dated for several months without any sexual contact at all, and Jordan still wasn't interested in showing affection, yet Cody was undeterred. After a year of dating, he asked her to marry him. To Cody's delight, she said "yes," and they started planning their wedding.

Jordan was clearly having second thoughts. She often asked her friends if she was making the right decision. Her friends could tell she was apprehensive, but she continued to plan the wedding regardless. Before the wedding, Jordan confided in her friends that she was excited about the wedding, but she wasn't looking forward to being married.

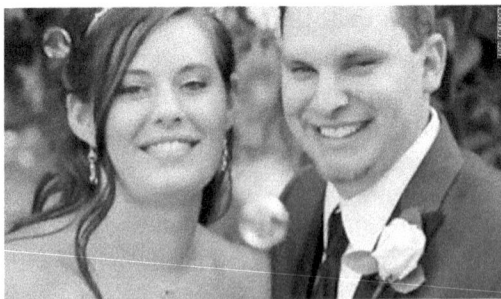

Jordan Graham & Cody Johnson

June 29, 2013, was the big day. It was a warm summer day in Montana. Cody and the wedding guests were excited, but Jordan's mood was somber and emotional. Walking down the aisle, Jordan was crying and looking at the ground. It was obvious that her tears weren't tears of joy; she was terrified. When Jordan got to the altar, the crying continued. She couldn't even look Cody in the eye. She held his hand but could only look at the ground in front of her.

After the ceremony, the newlyweds danced to a song composed by a friend, with lyrics,

> "...you helped me to climb higher for a better view... you're my safe place to fall...."

It was clear that Jordan didn't enjoy the wedding, the reception, or the thought of being married, and she was dreading what was coming next: the wedding night. She sent a text to her matron of honor:

> "I should be happy, and I'm just not."

> "I just know he's gonna want to do stuff, and I'm not really wanting to."

> "I'm using the 'my period started' spiel tonight. I freaking hope it works. Because if I'm forced to do something, I'm goin' to freak out."

> "I feel like it's my job to make him happy, even if I'm miserable."

In the days after the wedding, Jordan confessed to friends that they still hadn't consummated the marriage. She told them she was just too nervous and couldn't do it. While she was with friends, she was lethargic and depressed.

Cody also confided to his friends. He told them that even though they were now married, there was still no sex or even affection. Nothing had changed.

A week after their wedding, Jordan sent a text to a friend again,

> Jordan: "Oh well, I'm about to talk to him."
>
> Friend: "I'll pray for you guys."
>
> Jordan: "But dead serious, if you don't hear from me at all again tonight, something happened."

And something did happen. Nine days after the wedding, Cody's friends and family became worried when he didn't show up for work. That was entirely out of character for Cody. The last time anyone had seen him was with Jordan on Sunday afternoon after church at the local Dairy Queen.

When Cody's friends spoke to Jordan, she seemed unconcerned about Cody's disappearance. In fact, she was happy – happier than her friends had ever seen her.

Jordan told Cody's friends that he was out in the garage of their home that Sunday evening, then when she went out to see him, he wasn't there anymore. Instead, she saw a dark-colored car with Washington plates driving away. She claimed that she later got a message from him, saying he was going for a ride with friends from out of town.

Despite Jordan's story, Cody's friends knew he wouldn't just take off like that. He certainly wouldn't ignore their texts and calls. Knowing something was wrong, Cody's friends called the police and reported him missing.

Understandably, the first person that police wanted to speak to was the last person to have contact with him: his wife of little over a week, Jordan Graham.

Jordan told the police the same story she told Cody's friends. She claimed Cody had gone out for a drive with some of his buddies.

> "Well, I got a message saying that he was going to go for a ride with some of his out-of-town buddies that were visiting . . . I had no idea who they were . . . But he always told me this one thing, when his friends came to visit, he would take them to Glacier Park."

When asked if she and Cody had been fighting that night, she told police they hadn't. She had also told one of her friends that they hadn't been fighting. When the detectives eventually questioned all her friends, however, one friend had a conflicting story.

When questioning Jordan's matron of honor, Kimberly, they found that Jordan had told her that she and Cody had indeed been fighting. She said Cody had held her down while they argued, and he'd grabbed his keys and scratched her.

Friends and family showed up at Jordan's house to help her look for Cody, but she had no interest in looking for him. Instead, she became frustrated that everyone was so concerned about Cody. She was visibly flustered and, at one point, took off her wedding ring and threw it across the room. Her friends were shocked and confused. They wanted to help her find her husband, but she seemed to want the opposite.

Police noted Jordan's strange actions and the conflicting stories she had been giving. She seemed to give everyone involved a slightly different story. Even her friends were becoming suspicious of her and had no idea why she was behaving so strangely.

Then Jordan suddenly had some news. She told her friends that she'd gotten an email from someone who called himself "Tony the car man." In Tony's email, he wrote that Cody took him to Glacier National Park, and he accidentally fell off a cliff.

> "Hello Jordan, my name is Tony. There is no bother looking for Cody anymore. He's gone."

Her friends thought it was odd that Jordan had shown the email to them but not the police. What they thought was even more strange was that she wasn't crying. Someone had just told her that her husband of a little over a week was dead and she didn't seem the slightest bit upset. Her friend insisted that she show the email to detectives.

Investigators, of course, were immediately suspicious. They weren't suspicious of the mysterious "Tony" and the oddly worded email, but they were wary of Jordan. Detectives knew things just didn't happen that way. There was also the question of her demeanor. It was as if she was relieved by the message rather than saddened. Kalispell Police Detective Cory Clarke told reporters,

> "The email that she provided to us stated that these unknowns that he had taken off with, as well as this Tony person, had seen him fall from a cliff or at least disappear and that she was given explicit instructions to tell the police to call off the search. There was no more need to search for him, and at that point, I think she expected us to just walk away from it."

Four days after Cody's disappearance, she gathered her friends and told them she wanted them to help her look for Cody in Glacier National Park.

Glacier National Park is a massive park that spans over 1 million acres of rugged mountain terrain and has over 700 lakes. As she and her friends drove to the park, Jordan acted like it was a vacation. She drove with her arm out of the window, playing with the breeze and singing along to the songs on the radio. Her friends were sad and confused at her lack of emotion.

When they arrived at the park, her friends diligently searched as best as they could in such a gigantic park, but Jordan was barely making an effort. After a day of searching, they found nothing and drove back home.

The following day, they went to the park again. Within minutes of entering the park, Jordan knew precisely where to go. She told her friends that she thought he was at a particular spot on a trail called the Loop Trail. Along the Loop was a spot with a 300-foot cliff on the other side of a safety wall. Jordan seemed excited and said, "I think he's down here." She hopped over the safety wall and climbed to the cliff's edge, where she could see the bottom. She then yelled to her friends, "He's down there. I can see him!"

Jordan's friends were in disbelief. In a park that spans 13,000 square miles, she knew exactly where to go. When the police arrived, they used a helicopter to get to the bottom of the cliff. At the bottom, they found the body of Cody Johnson in the shallow water beneath a waterfall. Cody's body had extensive damage to his head and arms. It was determined that he had fallen face-first. His forehead had an eight-inch gash, and he was found without his wedding ring.

Aside from relief, Jordan was once again void of emotion. When police asked her how she knew where to find him in such a massive area, she replied,

> "The Holy Spirit led me to where he was. It was a place he had wanted to see before he died."

After only a few days of marriage, Jordan Graham was a widow, and she didn't seem to care. She told her friend, Kimberly,

> "Now that we have the body, we can have the funeral, and the cops can be out of it."

Jordan naively thought the police would just drop everything once his body was found.

By the time of Cody's funeral, just sixteen days after the wedding, there was no question in her friends' minds that Jordan was responsible for Cody's death. Jordan's behavior was simply unacceptable, and she showed no emotion at all. During the funeral, as they put Cody's body into the ground, his friends and family were crying, but Jordan was on her phone, texting. That only solidified her friends' suspicions. The police had felt the same and were building their case against Jordan.

After the funeral, Kalispell police brought her back in for more questioning. By this time, the FBI was involved. When agents told her that she was under arrest for killing her husband just eight days after their wedding, Jordan was unmoved. It wasn't until they presented with their evidence against her that she showed any emotion.

Police had subpoenaed Jordan and Cody's cell phone providers. The cell phone records showed they both entered Glacier National Park that Sunday evening. In addition, the security camera at the entrance to the park showed them entering the park in her car.

Police also proved that the email from "Tony the car man" was actually composed by Jordan at her stepfather's home. She had written the email herself to try and hide the crime.

After FBI agents presented the evidence against her, she broke down. She admitted that she had regrets about the marriage and was overwhelmed with negative emotions. She explained that they had been arguing on the night of Cody's death and decided to go to Glacier National Park and the Loop Trail. Jordan then mentioned something that shocked the FBI agents. Out of the blue, Jordan claimed that Cody told her that he knew the trail so well that he could wear a blindfold.

> "I didn't want to do that trail because I was afraid that he could fall, and he said, 'I could do it with a blindfold on. I could just put it on, take a step, and I wouldn't even fall.'"

This shocked them because police found a black cloth near the body that they believed could have been used as a blindfold. When tested by FBI forensic scientists, human hairs were embedded in it. Unfortunately, however, because the cloth was mishandled during the investigation, they were unable to prove that she had used it as a blindfold.

Additionally, on the Sunday before his disappearance, Cody's friends told police that he had been in a good mood because Jordan had told him she had a surprise. Cody and his friends all assumed that surprise was that they would finally have sex. With this information, FBI agents believed that Jordan brought Cody to the park, blindfolded him, and filled him with the hope that they would finally have sex.

Jordan explained that while on the Loop Trail, they hopped over the safety wall and climbed down a steep, rocky slope. They then made their way to the edge of a cliff with a massive drop below,

> "It kept going through my head that, you know, 'you are going to fall or something,' and then we were arguing some more, and he went to grab my arm and my jacket, and I said, 'no, I am going to defend myself.' So I said, 'let go,' and I pushed, and then he went over."

> "I wasn't thinking about where we were; I just pushed. I don't feel like I killed him; I mean, I pushed him, but it was an accident."

> "I think it's because emotions were running so high. I was frustrated, I was angry, I was every emotion I could ever think of all at once. And I've never felt like that before. I've never experienced such high emotions."

Later in the interrogation, she finally admitted that she had shoved Cody with both hands on his back in a fit of rage. Then, after he fell 300 feet to his death, she simply left the park and went home. On the one-hour drive home, she sent text messages to friends but mentioned nothing about what had just happened to her husband. She then made up stories to her friends and family that Cody had gone on a joyride with his friends.

Twenty-two-year-old Jordan Graham was charged with first-degree murder, second-degree murder, and making misleading statements to police. She faced a potential life sentence.

Initially, she pleaded not guilty, then changed her plea during the trial just before the case was presented to the jury. She pleaded guilty to second-degree murder and was sentenced to thirty years in prison without the possibility of parole.

Jordan Graham offered no apologies or explanations for her crime,

> "It was a moment of complete shock and panic. I have no other explanation."

> "I kinda was feeling, 'should we have waited a little bit longer and then got married?' I wasn't feeling like I was on cloud nine."

CHAPTER 12
THE LADY KILLER

Neville Heath was born on June 6, 1917, to a modest barber and his wife in Essex, England. The first school Neville attended allowed the "caning" of children as a form of punishment. It's assumed that at this early age is when Neville Heath acquired his fascination for sadomasochism. At age six, he stole one of his teacher's canes and beat a young girl with it.

The Heath family saved every penny so their son could go to Rutlish Grammar School, a well-known private school with famous former pupils including former British Prime Minister John Major.

Despite proper schooling, Neville didn't excel academically. Instead, at fifteen, he trapped a teenage girl in a room with him, kissed her, and held her throat tight enough to leave red scratch marks.

When he was seventeen years old, Neville Heath left his home in Ilford, England, and joined the Royal Air Force. Within a year, Heath had become a flying officer stationed in

Duxford. During his time in the military, he realized that women would pay more attention to him if he were wealthy and successful. Neville also knew that if he couldn't achieve riches and success, he could always fake it.

Heath forged checks and embezzled from the military to pay for a more extravagant lifestyle. When caught by military police, he escaped and stole a sergeant's car. He was quickly captured again and dismissed from the military for being absent without leave. He spent time defending himself in court for fraud and robbery charges and was sent to a Borstal school.

Heath was also well-known for impersonating various aristocrats. Some of his favorite fictitious names to use were Lieutenant-Colonel Armstrong and Lord Dudley. He used the money he stole from the military to pay for prostitutes that he hired to whip him.

Banishment from the military didn't deter Heath. He enjoyed military life, and one year later, he applied to join the Royal Army Service Corps. Unfortunately, World War II was imminent; the army willingly accepted him, turning a blind eye to his prior offenses.

In March 1940, Heath was commissioned to the Middle East and given the rank of second lieutenant, where he fought against Italian troops moving into Egypt. He was eventually promoted to acting captain.

Neville Heath

The war didn't keep him from continuing his deviant activities. During his time in the Middle East, he frequented brothels that let customers whip a girl for £50 per night. Somehow, he obtained an additional playbook which allowed him to be paid twice for his military service. He passed more bad checks and tried to con his superior officers. Finally, he was arrested but escaped, then was caught again and court-martialed.

Heath was placed in a troopship headed back to Britain. However, as the ship was sailing around the Cape of Good Hope, he jumped ship while docked in Durban, South Africa. In Durban, he started a new life and gave himself a new name: Captain Selway MC of the Argyll and Sutherland Highlanders.

While in South Africa, he met a girl named Elizabeth Pitt-Rivers. She came from a wealthy family, and when she became pregnant, he asked her to marry him. They had a son named Robert.

Under the name Armstrong, Heath joined the South African Air Force and became a bomber pilot, but he was eventually sent back to the Royal Air Force. On May 24, 1944, he was piloting a bomber between the Dutch and German border when it was hit by anti-aircraft fire. Heath bravely allowed his crew to bale out of the plane while he stayed at the control until the last moment, then parachuted to safety.

He returned to South Africa the following year, but inevitably faced yet another court-martial. This time it was for wearing decorations on his uniform that he didn't earn. Heath was finally dismissed from the military for a third time in February 1946 and returned to London.

––––––

The war had just ended, and the nightlife in London was back in full swing. Heath was now a handsome twenty-nine-year-old regular at the Soho and Kensington nightclubs. He was tall, good-looking, charming, and always had a girl on his arm. It was no problem for him to find girls that enjoyed the same fetishes he had.

One such girl was named Margery Gardner. Margery was a thirty-two-year-old divorcee who was an aspiring actress and had been an extra in a few British films. Heath and Margery met at the Panama Club in Kensington, and together, they frequented the hot nightspots of London and stayed in nearby hotels. On one occasion, another patron alerted the hotel manager to the screams of their bondage games.

On the evening of June 20, 1946, Neville Heath and Margery Gardner checked into the Pembridge Court Hotel in Notting Hill under the name Lieutenant Colonel Heath.

The following morning, a chambermaid found Margery Gardener dead in room four. Her clothes were soaked with blood, and her ankles were tied together. Ligature marks on her wrists showed that her hands had also been bound, but the bindings were missing. There were seventeen whip marks on her back from a leather woven horse riding crop with a ferrule tip. Her nipples had been bitten entirely off, and a rough item was inserted into her vagina that had been twisted, causing bleeding. Her face and chin were bruised, presumably by a fist. Strangely, her face had been washed, but dried blood was still visible in her nostrils and eyelashes. Neville Heath was nowhere to be found.

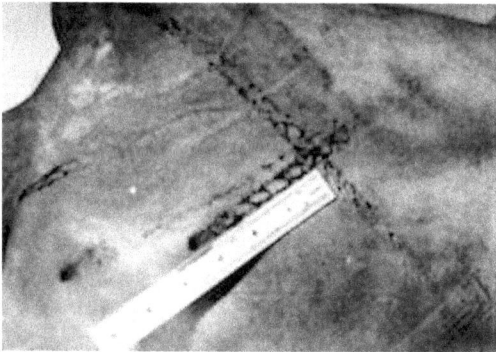

Whip marks on Margery Gardner's back

The coroner determined that Margery died from suffocation, not from her injuries. Both Margery and Heath were already in police files. Margery was known to associate with pimps and drug dealers and had recently been a passenger in a stolen car.

Police knew precisely who they were searching for, but Heath had fled to Worthing in Sussex. He was there to stay with a nineteen-year-old girl named Yvonne Symonds, who believed she was Heath's fiancée. Heath had met Yvonne just five days earlier in London, where he proposed marriage to her so that he could get her into bed.

Heath explained to Yvonne that he was indirectly involved in a murder and that the police may be looking for him. He told her he lent the hotel room to his friend, Margery Gardner, who was looking for somewhere to take a man she had met that night. When he returned to the room, he found Margery dead in the bed and left immediately. He told Yvonne, "the person that could do such a thing must be a sexual maniac." He then told Yvonne he was completely innocent and would go back to London and talk to Scotland Yard.

But Heath didn't go back to London. Instead, he wrote a letter to Superintendent Tom Barrett:

> "I feel it to be my duty to inform you of certain facts in connection with the death of Mrs. Gardner.
>
> I booked in last Sunday but not with Mrs. Gardner, whom I met for the first time during the week. I had drinks with her on Friday evening, and whilst I was with her, she met an acquaintance with whom she was obliged to sleep. The reasons as I understand them were mainly financial.
>
> It was then that Mrs. Gardner asked if she could use my hotel room until two o'clock and intimated that I might spend the remainder of the night with her. I gave her my keys.
>
> It must have been almost 3:00 a.m. when I returned to the hotel and found her in the condition of which you are aware. I realized that I was in an invidious position and packed my belongings and left.
>
> Since then, I have been in several minds whether to come forward or not, but in view of the circumstances, I have been afraid to.

I can give you a description of the man. He was aged approximately thirty, dark-haired with a small mustache. His name
was Jack. I gathered he was a friend of Mrs. Gardner of some
long-standing.

I have the instrument with which Mrs. Gardner was beaten,
and I'm forwarding this to you today. You will find my
fingerprints on it, but you should also find others as well.

NGC Heath"

Heath sent the letter but didn't include the riding crop. He
then left Worthing and traveled to Bournemouth, on the
southern coast of England. Bournemouth was busy in the
summer, with thousands of people soaking up the sun on the
beach. Heath checked into the Tollard Royal Hotel under the
name Group Captain Rupert Brooks.

Police had alerted the media that they were looking for
Neville Heath, but they hadn't presented a photo to the press.
Thus, Heath was able to stay in Bournemouth undetected
under an assumed name for thirteen days without attracting
attention.

———

Nineteen-year-old Doreen Marshall was vacationing in
Bournemouth with her friend, Peggy. Doreen was recovering
from a nasty bout of the flu, and her father had thought that
a little time in the sun would do her good. Doreen, a former
WREN (Women's Royal Navy Service), was walking along
the promenade when she met Group Captain Rupert Brooks,
Heath's latest assumed name.

Heath struck up a conversation by claiming he had previously met Peggy at a club. Peggy said she remembered him

out of courtesy, but she had no idea who he was. As the day progressed, it was clear that Heath had his eye on Doreen, so Peggy left the two alone for the rest of the afternoon.

Heath and Doreen spent the hot July 3rd walking around the town. They had tea at the Tollard Royal Hotel that evening and, later that evening, dinner and drinks.

At the end of the evening, Doreen asked the hotel to call her a cab back to her hotel, but Heath protested. It was a beautiful, warm night, and Heath insisted on walking her back to her hotel. She was staying at The Norfolk, a posh five-star hotel that her father had paid for, but Doreen never made it back.

The night porter at the Tollard Royal Hotel had worked the hotel's front door all night and knew that Group Captain Rupert Brooks had not returned. Concerned, the night porter checked his room at 4:00 a.m. and was surprised to find him safe and asleep inside.

The following morning, when questioned about how he got back into his room, Heath explained that he had played a joke on the night porter. As he returned from dropping off Doreen Marshall, he explained that he saw a ladder leading up to his room that a construction crew had left behind. He said he climbed the ladder back into his room and went to sleep.

———

Two days later, the management at The Norfolk was worried about their guest, Doreen Marshall. She hadn't shown up for daily meals in two days. The last they had seen her, she was getting into a taxi headed for the Tollard Royal Hotel. So, the manager of The Norfolk called the manager of the Tollard Royal.

The manager of the Tollard Royal had seen Doreen dining with Group Captain Rupert Brooke, aka Heath. He then informed Heath that the girl was missing and he should call the police.

Using his assumed name, Heath spoke to the police and told them that Doreen Marshall had been flirting with an American soldier earlier in the evening before she went missing, and he believed she might have gone off with him.

Detective Constable Souter questioned Heath and noticed he was a bit too calm about the situation. His smooth-talking demeanor didn't sit well with Souter.

Heath explained that he had walked Doreen part of the way home that night and dropped her off at the pier. He even claimed to have seen her the following day in the city. He repeated to the Detective that he had climbed the ladder outside his hotel to play a prank on the night porter, but this only made Souter more suspicious. He wondered if the real reason he used the ladder might have been because he didn't want the hotel staff to know what time he came back to the hotel.

Just as Heath left the police station, Doreen's father and older sister arrived. Heath was visibly shaken to meet them both but particularly her sister, who looked strikingly like Doreen. Souter noticed his nervousness and said, "Isn't your name Heath?" Heath replied, "Certainly not!" Souter continued, "But you look like the pictures in the papers." Heath replied, "I suppose I do."

What Heath didn't know was that there were no pictures in the papers. The police only released photos of Neville Heath to other police stations, not to the press. Souter alerted Scotland Yard, and on July 6, 1946, Heath was arrested in Bournemouth.

Upon Heath's arrival at the Bournemouth police station, he complained that he was cold. He had left his sports coat at the Tollard Royal Hotel, and he asked the police if they would pick it up for him. When detectives picked up his coat, they found three items in the pockets: a cloakroom receipt from Bournemouth Rail Station, the return half of Doreen Marshall's rail ticket, and a single, white, artificial pearl. Heath claimed he found the return railway ticket on a seat in the lounge of the Tollard Royal Hotel.

Police then took the cloakroom receipt to Bournemouth Rail Station and retrieved the suitcase that Heath had checked in. Inside the suitcase, they found a blue wool scarf stained with blood, a hat with the name "Heath" inside, and a riding crop. The riding crop had a diamond crisscross weave and a ferrule-like hard tip, similar to what had created the marks on Margery Gardner's back. The riding crop had been wiped clean but still had a small amount of blood on it. Police also believed the blue wool scarf might have been used to restrain or gag Margery Gardner.

Neville Heath was officially charged with Margery Gardner's death and taken to London, but Doreen was still missing in Bournemouth.

Two days after Heath's arrest, Kathleen Evans was walking her dog through Branksome Dene Chine, a park just west of the hotels in Bournemouth. Her dog was sniffing at something beneath a rhododendron bush. Beneath the bush, swarming with flies, Mrs. Evans found the body of Doreen Marshall, covered with a camel hair jacket.

Doreen's body was naked except for her left shoe. She had been bludgeoned, raped, and mutilated. She was slashed with a knife from her breast to her vagina. A rough object had torn her vagina and was inserted into her anus. Similar to Margery, one of Doreen's nipples had been bitten off. Her hand was sliced as if she'd tried to defend herself from a knife attack.

Her black dress and a makeup compact were found near her body. Also nearby was her broken artificial pearl necklace, with twenty-seven pearls scattered about. The twenty-eighth was the one found in Heath's coat pocket.

The knife was never found. Nor were Heath's bloody clothes. Police believed that, after he murdered her, he ran into the ocean to wash himself and threw the knife into the sea. They believed that he then went back to his hotel and climbed up the workman's ladder to avoid being seen by the night porter.

Heath originally wanted to plead guilty,

> "Why shouldn't I? After all, I did kill them."

But his attorney convinced him to enter a plea of not guilty by reason of insanity.

In England at that time, a person could only be tried for one crime at a time, so he was only tried for the murder of Margery Gardner. At the trial, women lined up for over ten hours outside the Central Criminal Court to catch a glimpse of "the most dangerous criminal modern Britain has known," as the newspapers described.

During the trial, Heath offered no reason for his killings, saying, "I felt my head go tight." The defense brought up evidence from Doreen's murder to emphasize their insanity plea, but their plan didn't work. The trial only lasted three days, and the jury took less than an hour to reach a verdict.

Neville Heath was found guilty and sentenced to death by hanging. While awaiting execution, Heath didn't seem to care about his fate. He spent his time in his cell reading *The Thirty-Nine Steps* several times and writing letters to his mother, in which he said,

> "My only regret is that I have been damned unworthy of you both."

Heath dressed up for his execution. When given the traditional shot of whiskey before execution, he held out his glass and said, "Old boy, considering the circumstances, you might make that a double."

Neville Heath was hanged in Pentonville Prison on October 16, 1946, just four months after the first murder. Within twenty minutes of his execution, Madame Tussaud's Wax Museum in London debuted its latest wax figure: Neville Heath.

CHAPTER 13
APPENDIX: LARRY GENE BELL

The following is the full transcript from the long, rambling telephone conversation from Thursday evening after Shari Smith's body was found. (Chapter 4)

———

Operator: "I have a collect call for Dawn Smith."

Beverly: "Dawn is not taking any calls. Could I have a name, please?"

Larry Gene Bell: "Put Dawn on the line please."

Beverly: "Dawn can't come to the phone right now. This is her Aunt Beverly."

Bell: "Well, may I speak to Mrs. Smith? This is an emergency."

Beverly: "Well, I'm sorry, she is being sedated and cannot come to the phone. She is asleep."

Bell: "Ok, may I speak to Bob Smith?"

Beverly: "Bob is up at the funeral home. You realize the situation with their daughter? Wait a minute, you asked to speak to Mrs. Smith?"

Bell: "Or Dawn, I'd rather speak to Dawn."

Beverly: "Uh, well, let me see if we can find her."

Bell: "Ok, hurry up."

Beverly: "Ok, they are looking for her right now."

Bell: "Thank you. Ok, thank you, operator. I'll speak to anybody that comes to the phone, now."

Beverly: "This is her Aunt Beverly."

Operator: "Collect from Joe Wilson. Will you accept the charge?"

Beverly: "Yes, we'll accept the charge. This is Shari's Aunt Beverly. I'll be happy to speak to you. Who am I speaking to please?"

Bell: "I want to speak to Dawn."

Beverly: "We're trying to locate her. In the meantime, I'll be happy to speak to you."

Bell: "No, thank you. I'll have to go then if I can't talk to her."

Beverly: "She's coming. Wait one moment, please. She went outside to walk the dog. They are looking for her. Ok, here's Dawn right now."

Dawn Smith: "Hello."

Bell: "Dawn?"

Dawn: "Yes."

Bell: "I'm calling for Shari Faye. Are you aware that I'm turning myself in tomorrow morning?"

Dawn: "No."

Bell: "Well, have you talked to Sheriff Metts or Charlie Keyes?"

Dawn: "Uh, no."

Bell: "Well, talk to them and listen carefully. I have to tell you this, Shari asked me to uh, turn myself in on the fifth day after they found her."

Dawn: "Wait, I'm trying to write this down."

Bell: "Don't write it down. I, uh, got to get myself straight with God and uh, turn myself completely over to him."

Dawn: "Ok."

Bell: "And uh, Charlie Keyes…you'll know what I'm talking about when you talk to him. He will not be able to get a personal interview from me in the morning. I'm uh, there'll be a letter. It's already been mailed. An exact copy for you and for him and it's with pictures."

Dawn: "A copy for me?"

Bell: "Yes, and him at his home of pictures of Shari Faye from the time I made her stand up to her car and took two pictures and all through the thing, and the letter will describe exactly what happened from the time I picked her up until the time, uh, I called and told y'all where to find her."

Dawn: "Ok."

Bell: "And I'll be doing the same in the morning at 6:00 a.m. and tell the sheriff and Charlie Keyes. I used him as a medium today and talked to him."

Dawn: "Ok, at 6:00 a.m., what will you be doing in the morning?"

Bell: "Well, he'll know."

Dawn: "He'll know?"

Bell: "Ok, and also that uh, uh, that I will be armed, but by the time they find me, I won't be dangerous. Do you understand that?"

Dawn: "You will be armed?"

Bell: "But by the time they find me, I won't be dangerous."

Dawn: "What does that mean?"

Bell: "Well, I…Shari Faye said if I couldn't live with myself, and she wouldn't forgive me if I didn't turn myself in or turn myself over to God, so I'm going to have to…this thing got out of hand, and all I wanted to do was make love to Dawn. I've been watching her for a couple of…"

Dawn: "To who?"

Bell: "To…I'm sorry, to Shari. I watched her a couple of weeks and uh, it just got out of hand and Dawn, Dawn, I hope you and your family forgive me for this."

Dawn: "You're not going to kill yourself, are you?"

Bell: "I…I can't live in prison and go to the electric chair. I can't do that. This is the only way I can get myself straight. I'm very sick, and I can't go through…"

Dawn: "We don't want you to die. We want to help you. Don't kill yourself."

Bell: "No, I just uh, you can't take someone's life, and this is the way it's going to have to be. Shari said…"

Dawn: "But listen to me, ok?"

Bell: "Well, listen I have to go."

Dawn: "No, I've got to tell you something. This is important."

Bell: "Well, these calls are being traced."

Dawn: "But God can forgive you and erase all of that."

Bell: "Dawn, I can't…I can't live with myself."

Dawn: "And we can forgive you, too."

Bell: "I can't live in prison for the rest of my life or go to the electric chair."

Dawn: "Listen, Shari is at peace with God. She's better off than any of us."

Bell: "Well, I want to say something to you that she told me."

Dawn: "Ok."

Bell: "Shari…oh, boy. Shari Faye said that uh…she did not cry the entire time, Dawn. She was very strong-willed and she said that uh, she did not want y'all to ruin your lives… and to go on with your lives like the letter said. I've never lied to y'all before, right? Everything I've told you came through, right."

Dawn: "Yes."

Bell: "Ok, so this is going to have to be the way it is, and she said that uh, she wasn't scared…that she knew that she was going to be an angel, and if I took the latter choice that she suggested to me, that she would forgive me, but our God's going to be the major judgment, and she'll probably end up seeing me in heaven, not in hell. And that uh, she requests… now please remember this. Now, she requests that y'all be sure to take her hands and fold them on her stomach like she's praying."

Dawn: "Ok."

Bell: "And that closed casket…"

Dawn: "Yeah."

Bell: "They already made those plans?"

Dawn: "Yes."

Bell: "Ok, and please have Charlie Keyes with Sheriff Metts, and Charlie knows what to do in the morning and have an ambulance and probably before they get there, they might as well have a hearse also and uh, and I'm just going to allow myself enough time to get in the area and get set up. I'm not in the area, now and uh, it'll be six in the morning that I'll call his office and by the time they reach me, I'll be straight with God and uh…Shari said please take the gold necklace that she had on, and she had one earring in her left ear."

Dawn: "Uh-huh."

Bell: "And uh, save those things and treasure them."

Dawn: "Save them?"

Bell: "Yes."

Dawn: "She doesn't want Richard to have that necklace?"

Bell: "Uh, she said something. There was some special jewelry in her room. I forgot what. It might have been the necklace. But uh, yeah, go, go ahead but the rest of her stuff is irrelevant."

Dawn: "What about her high school ring?"

Bell: "Uh, she said everything else would be decided by the family."

Dawn: "But Shari was not afraid, and she didn't cry or anything?"

Bell: "No, she didn't do anything. And I did make love to her and we had oral sex for uh, three different times and uh, can you handle it if I tell you how she died?"

Dawn: "Yes."

Bell: "Ok, now be strong, now."

Dawn: "Ok."

Bell: "She said you were strong. She told me all about the family and everything. We talked and...oh God...and I am a family friend. That's the sad part."

Dawn: "You are a family friend?"

Bell: "Yeah, and that is why I can't face y'all. You...you'll find out in the morning or tomorrow."

Dawn: "Yes."

Bell: "Ok, I tied her up to the bedpost and uh, with electric cord and uh, she didn't struggle, cry or anything. She let me voluntarily...from her chin to her head, ok, I'll go ahead and tell you. I took duct tape and wrapped it all the way around her head and suffocated her, and tell the coroner or get the information out how she died and uh, I was unaware she had this disease. I probably would have never taken her and uh, I shouldn't have took her, anyway. It just got out of hand and uh, I'd asked her out before, and she said she would if she wasn't going with anybody, and uh, she said also that uh…oh yeah, make sure Charlie Keyes…you know him, the reporter on WIS?"

Dawn: "I can't think of who he is right now."

Bell: "Ok, they'll know who he is. He's the one who wears the bow tie on Channel 10. He's the head news fellow on this case for Channel 10. And, oh yeah, I was there Saturday morning for the search."

Dawn: "You were at the search Saturday morning?"

Bell: "Yes, I was…and if…oh God, Dawn. I wish uh, I wish y'all could help me, but it's just too late. Well, I have to go, now, Dawn. I know the…"

Dawn: "Let me tell you something, ok? God can forgive you, and through God we can forgive you also."

Bell: "Well, uh, Dawn…will you forgive me then?"

Dawn: "Yes."

Bell: "Your family? But I'll have to take the other choice that Shari Faye said to me. I just can't live with myself like this. I'm not…"

Dawn: "I just think you need to think about that a little harder."

Bell: "I'm not going to be caged up like a dog. Ok, now, are there any other questions? I've got to go now. Time's running out."

Dawn: "Uh, when…when you killed Shari, was she at peace? She wasn't afraid or anything?"

Bell: "She was not, she was at peace. She knew that God was with her and she was going to become an angel."

Dawn: "And she wrote that letter to us of her own free will and all that was…"

Bell: "She sure did. Everything I've told y'all has been the truth. Hasn't everything come true?"

Dawn: "Yes, it has. Can…can I ask you one more question?"

Bell: "One more and that's it."

Dawn: "You told us that Shari was kidnapped at gunpoint?"

Bell: "Yeah."

Dawn: "But she knew you?"

Bell: "Yeah. At first, see, I pulled up and uh, I'm telling you the truth. I have no reason to lie to y'all. I've always told you the truth, right?"

Dawn: "Right."

Bell: "Ok, and I had her…asked her to stand there and took two instant pictures."

Dawn: "You asked her to stand where?"

Bell: "At the mailbox with her car in the background. These pictures, detailed pictures will be with…with the letter that you receive. Since I'm out of town…probably not 'til Saturday. And Charlie Keyes will get a copy and your family will get a copy, and it's addressed to you unless the mail holds it up."

Dawn: "So she didn't realize that you were going to kidnap her?"

Bell: "That's exactly right. And uh, what else? So tell Sheriff Metts that it's no use in uh…trying to trace these calls to catch me. It's too late now. I won't be taken alive. And also, Dawn, that uh, uh, he can just call off the damn search. It's over now, and I don't want the people out there wasting their time, and everything I've told you is true and this is coming true, also. I just can't live with it. I can't take it anymore. Shari Faye was right. We, I feel like I got close to her and we…she showed me things. She was very…"

Dawn: "Why are you talking to me instead of mom?"

Bell: "She felt like you were strong-willed more than your mother."

Dawn: "Oh, did you start talking to her?"

Bell: "Uh, she said it was your aunt, but it was your mother, correct?"

Dawn: "Uh, no, that was my aunt that answered the phone."

Bell: "Oh, it was? Ok. She said something about your mother being under medication. Shari Faye told me. Remember I told you on the fifth day to let them know where she was so her blessings of the body could be blessed. Right?"

Dawn: "Why on the fifth day did she want us to find her? Why not…"

Bell: "I don't know. She just…she just said that. I don't know. I don't have any idea. I'm telling you exactly how she died, so she died of suffocation. And so…ok anything else?"

Dawn: "Why did you…why did you do that?"

Bell: "She…I gave her a choice…to shoot her or give her a drug overdose or suffocate her."

Dawn: "Why did you have to kill her?"

Bell: "It got out of hand. I got scared because, uh, only God knows, Dawn. I don't know why. God forgive me for this, I hope. And I got to straighten it out or he'll send me to hell, and I'll be there the rest of my life, but I'm not going to be in prison and electric chair."

Dawn: "But I don't think taking your life is the answer to this."

Bell: "I'll think about it. Well, Dawn, I've got to go now. It's been too long and, uh, tell them to just forget about the search. I'll be in the area long enough in the morning for them to, uh, find me, and by the time I call, uh Charlie Keyes will know exactly the set-ups. I hope now, uh, I know why I'm staying on the phone. They are taping this, right?"

Dawn: "Uh-huh."

Bell: "Ok, good, and anything else? Oh, yeah. Let me tell you. The other night they almost caught me. The ignorant son-of-a-guns, I wanted them to catch me. I felt that way at the time, but now…"

Dawn: "When…when was this?"

Bell: "Uh, when I called at 9:45."

Dawn: "When you were over near Jake's Landing?"

Bell: "Yeah, I was at that Fast Fare thing."

Dawn: "Yeah."

Bell: "I pulled out twenty yards in front of two flashing lights."

Dawn: "What color car did you have?"

Bell: "They hit it dead on it, red, and they didn't even... Dawn, I can't get over this. Them ignorant so-and-sos didn't even turn around and follow me, and I cut right at that blinking light down there to go the back way on Old Cherokee Road. And there was a highway patrolman or somebody in front of me and pulled the car in front of me, and he let me turn right on Old Cherokee Road. Can you believe that?"

Dawn: "So, you really wanted to be caught?"

Bell: "At that time, but it's too late, now."

Dawn: "What kind of car was it?"

Bell: "Oh, well, they came mighty damn close. Dawn, they're not going to catch me, and I can't give you information because I got to make it back in time, and they'll stop me before I get back if I tell you, but they're right, it was a red one, and I almost got caught three or four times."

Dawn: "Was it a red Jetta?"

Bell: "Dawn, that's irrelevant now. If I die now, or if I die at six o'clock in the morning, it's irrelevant. Well, listen, Dawn."

Dawn: "I really wish you would just think about not killing yourself."

Bell: "And Shari told me to tell you, please go back to Carowinds. I know you live in Charlotte, and, uh, I know a lot about family, and uh, go back and start singing and give it your best, and that she knows that she'll be singing like crazy. When she said that, she was smiling."

Dawn: "She was smiling and she wasn't afraid the whole time?"

Bell: "No, never."

Dawn: "Because she knew that she was going to be with God."

Bell: "That's exactly right, the whole time, the whole time. She's so damn strong-willed, and, and…"

Dawn: "But, I just wish you would think about not killing yourself."

Bell: "I will, Dawn."

Dawn: "Listen, our prayers will be for you."

Bell: "I'll call you collect…will be for you, ok. Will you be home tonight?"

Dawn: "We are home tonight. Listen, our prayers will be with you, ok? God can do anything and he can forgive you for this."

Bell: "Yeah, but you know what's going to happen to me, Dawn? I'm going to be fried."

Dawn: "You don't know that. God can work miracles. You don't know that'll happen to you. God is merciful no matter what we do."

Bell: "It's time now, it's time. I got to go now, and I'll just…I'll think about it, but I've got a lot of things on my mind, now. I know you know that, right?"

Dawn: "Right."

Bell: "And, uh, you answer the phone every time it rings tonight."

Dawn: "Me answer the phone tonight, every time it rings?"

Bell: "That's right, and if it's collect, and I'll say, Dawn, like the break of day, you'll know."

Dawn: "Ok, now if we're asleep, you let it keep ringing, ok?"

Bell: "I will, I will. Ok, well, God bless us all."

Dawn: "Wait, mother wants to say something to you."

Bell: "All right, just one thing and then I'm gone."

———

Hilda Smith: "Hello."

Bell: "Just say one thing and that's it. Dawn will tell you, and you listen to the recordings and there will be a letter you'll receive probably the next day with pictures and detailed information from the time I picked Shari up at the mailbox up 'til tonight and my departure from this earth. Sheriff Metts might as well call it off. It's over. I will not be taken alive. Dawn told me to turn myself in or turn myself over to God, or I'll never live in peace and never be forgiven and go to heaven."

Hilda: "Well, turn yourself over to God. That's most important."

Bell: "I am and this is the only way. I'm not going to spend my life in prison and go to the electric chair. Well, uh, Dawn knows everything and, uh, God bless all of us and I hope…"

Hilda: "Listen, I want to ask you something."

Bell: "This just got out of hand. This got out of hand…"

Hilda: "All you had to do was let her go."

Bell: "I was scared. She, she, was dehydrating so damn bad."

Hilda: "You could have called me for medicine. I would have met you anywhere."

Bell: "Well, that's irrelevant now."

Hilda: "I mean all you had to do was let her go. Such a beautiful young life…"

Bell: "I know that. That's why I have to join her now, hopefully, and uh, Mrs. Smith, please, uh, ok, well, that's it. I got to go."

Hilda: "Did she know you when you stopped?"

Bell: "Yeah, uh, I took two pictures, instamatic of, I made her stand…well, before she knew I was going to kidnap her, I asked her to stand at the mailbox, and you'll see by the picture…her car door. I think there's about eight pictures and Charlie Keyes will be receiving a set and a detailed letter, like I told you, at his house, if this mail doesn't slow it down, which it probably will. If you don't get it tomorrow, you'll get it the next day. You'll get exact copies, the pictures that he gets and, uh, exact letters, too."

Hilda: "Do you know all of us or just Shari?"

Bell: "I know the whole family unfortunately, that's why I can't face you. Ok, well, Mrs. Smith, please, uh, if I decide different, I've already told Dawn what's going to happen. Her answer the phone tonight only, and it will be collect, and I'm going to allow myself just enough time to get back in the area to set everything up if you don't hear from me tonight. I knew the calls were traced, and they came real close to catching me three or four different times and they are correct, I am in a red vehicle."

Hilda: "What kind?"

Bell: "I'm sorry, I don't want them to catch me before I meet my maker on Judgment Day."

Hilda: "You think the maker's going to forgive you now?"

Bell: "He'll, he'll do that, or I'll be crucified and go to hell."

Hilda: "That's right."

Bell: "Well, I've got a lot to think about and I'm, I'm gone Mrs. Smith, and uh, please, I know this might be selfish, but, uh, you all please, ask a special prayer for me? Your, your daughter said that she was not afraid, and she was strong-willed. She, uh, knew that she was going to heaven, was going to be an angel, and like I told Dawn, she was going to be singing like crazy and when she said that she was smiling."

Hilda: "Did you tell her you were going to kill her?"

Bell: "Yes, I did and I gave her the choice, like, it's on the recording. I asked her if she wanted it to be drug overdose, shot or, uh, uh, suffocated, and she picked suffocation."

Hilda: "My God, how could you?"

Bell: "Well, forgive us, God."

Hilda: "Not us, you."

Bell: "God only knows why this happened. I don't know. It just got out of hand."

Hilda: "I thought you were considerate and loving and a kind person."

Bell: "Goodbye, Mrs. Smith."

———

The next segment is the phone call that occurred immediately after Shari Smith's funeral:

Operator: "I have a collect call for Dawn Smith from Shari, will you pay for the call?"

Dawn: "From who?"

Operator: "Shari."

Dawn: "Yes."

Operator: "Go ahead, please."

Larry Gene Bell: "Is this Dawn Smith, like the break of day?"

Dawn: "Yes, it is."

Bell: "Ok, you know this is not a hoax call, correct?"

Dawn: "Yes."

Bell: "Ok, did I catch you off guard?"

Dawn: "Well, yeah, because they said it was from Shari."

Bell: "No, I said concerning Shari. Everybody's screwed up here. Excuse my French. Ok, listen carefully."

Dawn: "Ok."

Bell: "Uh, Dawn, I'm real afraid, now and everything and…"

Dawn: "You're what?"

Bell: "Real afraid, and I have to, uh, make a decision. I'm going to stay in this area until God gives me the strength to decide which way…and I did go to the funeral today."

Dawn: "You did?"

Bell: "Yes, and uh, that ignorant policeman…the fellow even directed me into a parking space. Blue uniform…outside, and they were taking license plate numbers down and stuff. Please tell Sheriff Metts I'm not jerking anybody around, I'm not playing games, this is reality and I'm not an idiot. When he finds my background, he'll see I'm a highly intelligent person."

Dawn: "Uh-huh."

Bell: "Ok, and I want to fill in some gaps here because now and next Saturday, the anniversary date of Shari Faye."

Dawn: "Yeah."

Bell: "I'm going to do one way or the other, or if God gives me strength before then, ever when, and I'll call you."

Dawn: "Between now and next Saturday?"

Bell: "Yes."

Dawn: "I think you need to make a decision before then."

Bell: "All right, and uh, I could tell her casket was closed, but did y'all honor Shari's request for folding her hands?"

Dawn: "Yes, yes we did, of course."

Bell: "Ok, she'll, she'll like that. That'll please her. Ok, and uh, tell Sheriff Metts and the FBI, damn, that's like the fear of God in you for sure. They treat this like Bonnie and Clyde. They go out and gun you down, and if I decide, if God gives me the strength to just surrender like that, I'll call you, like I said. When I see them drive up, I'll see Charlie Keyes and Sheriff Metts get out of the car, they'll recognize me. I'll approach them, and I'll put my hands straight up in the air and turn my back to them, and they can approach me without shooting me and stuff, all right? I delivered her to Saluda County, I told you exactly how she died and so forth, and when I took the duct tape off of her, it took a lot of hair with it and so, that'll help 'em out. The examiner said they were having problems telling how she died. And, uh...well, hold on a minute now and let's see..."

Dawn: "Where's the duct tape?"

Bell: "Huh?"

Dawn: "Where's the duct tape?"

Bell: "Only God knows, I don't...ok, ok, now listen. Did you receive the thing and the pictures in the mail?"

Dawn: "They're coming?"

Bell: "Unless the FBI intercepts them. It's written to you. I got Shari Faye to address three or four different things, and it's written to you in her handwriting."

Dawn: "What is written to me?"

Bell: "It's addressed to you. Ok, and now, she, she gave me your address in Charlotte, and there's one picture she wanted me to send to you, and you'll get that in about a week or so, to your Charlotte address and it's...this little note is for your eyes only in her handwriting and she said, Richard, don't tell him this, it'll break his heart. She was getting ready to break up with him, because he was over jealous and that, uh, she couldn't go anywhere and talk to any fellows without him arguing with her, and every time he'd come down to the flea market where she worked in the concession stand, he'd get mad because she couldn't talk to him and working. He worked and we talked from, uh, actually she wrote the 'Last Will and Testament,' 3:12 a.m. She kind of joked and said they won't mind if I round it off to 3:10. So, from about two o'clock in the morning from the time she actually knew until she died at 4:58, we talked a lot and everything, and she picked the time. She said she was ready to depart. God was ready to accept her as an angel."

Dawn: "So, the whole time, you told her that she was going to die, right?"

Bell: "Yeah, ok…and uh, all those times and stuff I gave you before were correct and accurate, ok. When are you going to go back to Charlotte and get the letter? Whenever I get strength, and God shows me which way, I'll mail it like a couple of hours before."

Dawn: "Ok, where is Shari's high school ring?"

Bell: "Uh, Shari's high school ring was not with her."

Dawn: "It was not with her?"

Bell: "No, not unless it was in her car or her pocketbook."

Dawn: "She always wears that ring, and if it was, please, you know…"

Bell: "I'm telling you the truth."

Dawn: "The family would really like to have it."

Bell: "I'm returning everything. I mean I don't have anything of Shari's. I don't have that. If I had it, I'd mail it to you. I'm not lying to you. Ok, you said that, uh…Listen, wait, hold on a minute, I'm not finished, now. We talked about it so much. I made clip notes afterward. Uh, she said to tell Robert Jr. That's the brother, right?"

Dawn: "Yeah."

Bell: "Ok, tell him to grow up and meet his goals and pick a sport out, and he's a big boy, and uh, excel in it."

Dawn: "Uh-huh."

Bell: "Ok, and then the last thing, oh yeah, for respect of your family, Shari Faye always told me to respect the family, and I didn't mail Charlie Keyes a set of pictures and letters. I want your family only. So when you find me, uh, if God gives me the strength, ever which way he decides, it'll be in a plastic bag on my body, on my person, because if the media got a hold of this they'll have a field day. I chose Charlie Keyes as a medium because I thought he was very level-headed, and he wouldn't let it get out of hand, and I can trust him, 'cause I kind of know him. Ok, uh, the last thing she said is… a song, she wouldn't tell me, she said, well, I have to keep some things secret with you, and she kind of chuckled. She said that Dawn would know on her birthday, which is what, June 12, or something?"

Dawn: "On Shari's birthday?"

Bell: "Yeah, June or August…she told me…"

Dawn: "It's June."

Bell: "Ok, well, ever when it is. I think she said the twelfth or something, but anyway, uh, she said to pick her favorite song, and just you and the family, uh, you sing it and, uh, she'll be listening, and uh, put some real feelings behind it. Ok, and let's see, she, dang, let's see, let me go back through it. Ok, I was at the search Saturday morning and also Tuesday morning. I showed up when they called the volunteers off."

Dawn: "You were there?"

Bell: "Yeah."

Dawn: "You were there Tuesday morning also?"

Bell: "Yeah."

Dawn: "Were you there last night?"

Bell: "No, but I was there for the funeral this morning. And, uh, they took license, still, I'm not a damn idiot. I never had any problems before, and it's just something that got out of hand and that's all."

Dawn: "Can I ask you something?"

Bell: "Ok, now ask questions, but hurry."

Dawn: "Uh, I know that you keep telling me that you're telling me the truth, but, uh, you did tell me that you would give yourself up at six o'clock this morning. Well, what happened?"

Bell: "I didn't have the strength."

Dawn: "What?"

Bell: "I didn't have the strength. I was scared. I'm scared as hell. I can't even hardly read my handwriting."

Dawn: "Well, listen."

Bell: "Hurry, I've got to go."

Dawn: "No matter what you've done, you know that Christ died for you so that you could be forgiven, and if you would give yourself up…"

Bell: "Do you know what would happen, Dawn? Do you realize Sheriff Metts…Sheriff Metts would give me help for a couple of months, and then they'd find out I'm sane, and then I'd get tried and sent to the electric chair…put in prison for the rest of my life. I'm not going to, uh…go to the electric chair."

Dawn: "You keep telling us to forgive you…you don't realize what you've put us through. How could you think about what would happen to yourself?"

Bell: "Ok, any other questions? I've filled in all the holes and everything. If the only reason you wouldn't get that letter today or probably Monday, is that the FBI intercepted it."

Dawn: "Can you tell me where her ring is? You really don't know where it is?"

Bell: "No, I don't, Dawn. I would send it to you if I did. I have no reason. I'm not asking for money, materialistic things. I don't have any reason for…she was not wearing a high school ring when she got in the car, so maybe she left it at the pool party she came from."

Dawn: "Uh, can you tell me? Where did Shari die?"

Bell: "I told you, 4:58 in the morning."

Dawn: "No, I know the time, where?"

Bell: "Saturday morning in, uh, Lexington County."

Dawn: "In Lexington County?"

Bell: "Uh-huh."

Dawn: "Where in Lexington County?"

Bell: "Anything else you want to ask me?"

Dawn: "That's what I'm asking you, where?"

Bell: "Uh, anything else?"

Dawn: "You won't answer that for me?"

Bell: "No."

Dawn: "You said anything I'd ask, you'd tell me."

Bell: "Ok, I'll tell you. Uh, number one. I don't know exactly the location. I don't know the name of the highway, 391 or something like that, but right next to the Saluda County line.

That's all I can tell you. Ok, anything else? I'm getting ready to go. At 4:58 in the morning, set your alarm wherever you are, and I'll call you. Can you hear me?"

Dawn: "Yes, this morning?"

Bell: "No, next Saturday, on the anniversary date. Ok, I'll call you and tell you the exact location, just like I did Shari Faye's."

Dawn: "I can't believe this because you've never been telling me the truth."

Bell: "Ok, I have. You believe everything because it is the truth. You go back and you go over everything."

Dawn: "I just feel that the best thing for you to do is give…"

Bell: "Well, Dawn, God bless us all."

CHAPTER 14
BONUS CHAPTER: THE FAMILY MURDERS

T his chapter is a **free bonus chapter** from True
Crime Case Histories: Volume 7

The River Torrens flows from the peaks of Mount Pleasant,
through the Adelaide Hills, to the Adelaide Plains and
supplies water to the city center of Adelaide, Australia,
before it continues into Gulf St. Vincent.

In the early 1970s, the area where the river flows through the
base of the foothills was a popular "beat" for gay men to
meet. Homosexuality was illegal at the time and South
Australia's Vice Squad regularly patrolled the area.

In May 1972, corrupt police officers confronted three gay
men, Roger James, Dr. George Duncan, and another man.
Rather than cite the men for their crimes, the officers threw
them in the rapid waters of River Torrens and left them to
drown. Throwing gay men into the river was a common

occurrence among the Vice Squad who considered it a "sport" and referred to the act as "flinging a poof."

Dr. George Duncan, a law lecturer at Adelaide University, drowned in the incident and was found 500 meters downstream. His death made him a martyr for gay rights activists in the area and the event helped repeal South Australia's anti-homosexuality laws.

The other two men were rescued that night with the help of a young man that was driving by. The young man was Bevan Spencer von Einem. von Einem drove the two men to the hospital and became a hero in Southern Australia. Although von Einem's first media appearance made him a hero, years later, he would return to the spotlight for much more sinister reasons.

———

Seven years later, sixteen-year-old Alan Barnes had spent the night at a friend's house in Adelaide. The following morning, a Sunday in June 1979, the teenager walked to Grand Junction Road to see if he could hitch a ride home. Hitchhiking had been common in the area at the time and was generally a safe way to get around the city. Although Alan was due home that Sunday afternoon, his parents allowed the boy his independence and didn't think too much of it when he hadn't returned home that day. When he hadn't arrived by Monday morning, however, Alan's mother knew something was wrong and called police.

Alan had long, blonde hair that stood out in a crowd. When police questioned people in the area, several remembered seeing him hitchhiking, but only one could provide any useful information. A motorist that had been driving on

Grand Junction Road that morning claimed to have seen Alan getting into a car with three or four people. Unfortunately, the person was unable to give a description of the car or its passengers.

The following Sunday, just one week after Alan went missing, a couple hiking in the Adelaide Foothills near the South Para Reservoir came across an object along a trail beneath a bridge. As they approached, they could tell it was the body of a young male. The body had been twisted and contorted.

When police arrived, they found the body of a boy they believed to be in his twenties. It appeared someone had thrown the body over the railing of the bridge above, hoping it would land in the water. Instead, the body hit the dirt.

The news reports that evening announced that the body of a young man in his twenties was found deceased. When Alan's mother heard the news, she knew it had to be her son. She called police and said, "He's not in his twenties. He's sixteen. And if you look at the back of his watch, you'll see an engraving. It was his Christmas present."

It was indeed Alan. A postmortem examination of his body showed that he had died on Friday night or Saturday morning, just hours before he was dumped. Since he had been gone a week, that left the last six days of his life unaccounted for. His body had been meticulously washed clean in an attempt to hide evidence and he had been dressed in clothes that were not his own.

A toxicology examination revealed a large dose of a potent sedative called Noctec in his system. The condition of his body led police to believe that he had been drugged, severely beaten, brutally tortured, and held captive in the days before his death. Alan had died from massive blood loss in and around his anus. He had been raped with a large object, believed to be a bottle, which perforated the inside of his rectum. Clearly, it was the work of a psychotic sexual sadist.

————

Two months later, in August 1979, a man fishing from a dock at Mutton Cove, just Northwest of Adelaide, noticed a pair of black trash bags floating in the water along the bank of the Port Adelaide River. Curious, he opened one of the bags and called police when he saw what looked like butchered human remains inside.

The bags had been placed in the water just a mile from where the river flowed into the ocean. The killer assumed the current would carry the bags into the open sea, but they had caught on a dock.

When detectives opened the bag, it was enough to bring seasoned officers to tears. The first bag contained a male torso with the chest cavity cut open. The organs had been removed from the torso and placed into smaller plastic bags. The severed legs and arms had been stripped of skin and muscle tissue and placed into the chest cavity. The head had been severed from the body and strangely wired to the chest.

A medical examination determined the victim died in a similar manner to Alan Barnes. He had been tortured and bled to death from anal injuries. He had been brutally raped with a bottle-shaped object which had perforated his rectum and anus. There was evidence of blunt force trauma to his head, but not enough to have caused death.

Alan Barnes / Neil Muir

The body was identified as Neil Muir, a twenty-five-year-old gay heroin user that was well known to police. Neil lived alone and had only been reported missing two days before the body was found. Detectives weren't quite sure how long he had been missing. Like Alan Barnes, Neil had been last seen on a Sunday. Both bodies had been discarded in or near water and both had died of blood loss from anal injuries. Though the similarities seem glaringly obvious in hindsight, the two murders weren't initially linked together.

————

Shortly after the body of Neil Muir was discovered, police received an anonymous phone call from someone that referred to himself as "Mr. B." The caller told detectives he believed that Bevan Spencer von Einem was responsible for the murders. von Einem's name was added to a list of leads, along with hundreds of others.

When detectives interviewed von Einem, he freely admitted
that he knew Neil Muir. The two of them had been lovers
four years earlier. von Einem claimed to have met with Neil
a few days before he went missing, but hadn't seen him since.
Although it was a significant finding, the information was
lost in the hundreds of other leads detectives needed to
follow up on.

————

Two years had gone by with very little development in either
murder. On February 27, 1982, nineteen-year-old Mark
Langley attended a friend's birthday party. After the party, he
and two friends went for a drive through the city. As they
drove near the River Torrens, Mark had an argument with
his friends, got out of the car, and told them he would walk
home. Mark's friends drove off, but it had been a petty argument and, just minutes later, his friends had a change of
heart. They turned around to pick him up, but Mark was
nowhere to be found. Assuming he had found a ride home,
they went home without him.

The following morning, Mark's father called the police to
report him missing. Mark's friends and family searched the
area where he was last seen, but he had simply vanished.
Divers were sent to search the River Torrens but found nothing. Nine days after Mark went missing, his body was found
in an area called Summertown at the base of Mount Lofty,
just east of Adelaide.

Unlike the other victims, Mark's body had no visible external
injuries. His clothes were clean, but his blue undershirt was
missing, as was his silver necklace with a zodiac pendant. He
died, however, just like the others—from massive blood loss
due to injuries to his anus and rectum caused by the inser-

tion of a bottle-shaped object. Also, similar to Alan Barnes, Mark's body had been washed clean before it was dumped.

Strangely, Mark's body had a small, recent, vertical surgical scar. Someone had performed surgery on him just below his navel, even taking the time to shave him before surgery. The wound was stitched closed with surgical thread and Johnson & Johnson surgical tape afterwards. Medical examiners and investigators believed the surgery was performed in order to retrieve an object that may have been caught in his intestines - possibly an object that the killer believed could have contained a fingerprint.

Like the victims before, Mark had been given alcohol and a massive amount of a sedative called Mandrax, more widely known as methaqualone or quaalude.

Detectives finally began to consider the possibility that the three murders were linked. As a result, they began looking into other missing person cases that may also have been related. That's when they noticed the case file of Peter Stogneff.

———

On August 27, 1981, exactly six months before Mark Langley's disappearance, fourteen-year-old Peter Stogneff made plans with a friend to skip school. Before he left home that morning, he dropped his school backpack in his garage and took the bus into the city to meet his friend. Peter's friend waited patiently at the local shopping mall, but Peter never showed. Later that evening, when Peter didn't return home, his parents called the police to report him missing. An extensive search ensued, but Peter had vanished without a trace. The only clue was a witness at

Tea Tree Plaza that claimed they saw the boy with an adult male.

Almost a year later in a small town just north of Adelaide, a farmer conducting a burn-off (a fire-management process used to encourage plant growth and reduce wildfires) discovered a human skeleton in the ashes. Unfortunately, any evidence that may have been at the scene was now charred. Using dental records, investigators determined it was the remains of Peter Stogneff. Although they were unable to determine an official cause of death, medical examiners could tell that the spine had been severed with a saw and his legs had been sawed just above the knees.

————

For the next fifteen months, the cases went nowhere. Police briefly thought they had found the killer: Dr. Peter Millhouse, a doctor who had known Neil Muir. Prosecutors brought a case against the man based on weak circumstantial evidence, but at trial he was easily acquitted. They were back to square one.

————

On a Sunday afternoon in July 1983, fifteen-year-old Richard Kelvin and his friend Boris were at a local park kicking around a soccer ball. Richard was a handsome, athletic boy with a steady girlfriend and got good grades in school. That afternoon, as a joke, he wore the family dog's collar around his neck as he played with Boris in the park.

Peter Stogneff / Richard Kelvin

When it was time to go home, the two boys walked to the bus stop and Richard waited as Boris caught his bus home. Richard began his walk home, less than a quarter of a mile from the bus stop, but he never made it. He had simply disappeared.

The case of Richard Kelvin's disappearance drew more attention in the media than the other cases. Richard was the son of a well-known local newscaster that worked for Channel 9. Richard had been wearing a Channel 9 t-shirt when he disappeared.

Initially, local police assumed Richard had simply run away from home. His frustrated parents protested and explained that Richard was a good kid; he would never run away from home. Police had wasted two days and Richard still hadn't returned home. That Tuesday, police finally began a door-to-door search of the area and came up with a clue.

A man living nearby that worked as a security guard told police that on the Sunday evening when Richard went missing, he heard shouting on the street near his home. He said he could hear arguing, cries for help, and car doors slamming on the street nearby. One voice sounded young, several others were adults, and one voice appeared to be that of a woman. Immediately after the argument, he heard the loud exhaust of a car speeding away. By the time he looked outside, the car was gone. Other neighbors in the area corroborated the same story. It appeared as though a group of people had abducted Richard.

The location from which Richard was abducted was just a few blocks from where Mark Langley was last seen. Police and media immediately suspected that Richard may have been abducted by the same killer or killers as the other four victims. Theories arose that he possibly was abducted by sexual deviants because of the dog collar he wore around his neck.

Because of Richard's high-profile father, the story became front-page news. Everyone in the area seemed to have theories about what had happened and the police were inundated with calls. Anonymous callers told police he was being held in a camper near the mountains while others claimed to have seen his death in a snuff film.

Finally, seven weeks after Richard vanished, a family walking through the forest near Mount Crawford, northeast of Adelaide, came across what they thought was someone lying in the bushes in a fetal position. The father assumed it may be a man that was injured, but it soon became obvious that it was a dead body. As soon as the man noticed his Channel 9 shirt and the dog collar, he knew it was the body of Richard Kelvin.

An autopsy revealed exactly the same cause of death as the others: massive blood loss from anal injuries. His body had been washed clean and redressed in his own clothes. Richard, however, had been missing for much longer than the others. The state of decomposition revealed that he had been dead for only a week in the scrub brush. That meant that Richard had endured five to six weeks of excruciating torture and sexual abuse before his death.

Like the others, Richard's body contained a massive cocktail of powerful sedatives including Noctec (Chloral Hydrate), Mandrax (Quaalude), Valium (Diazepam), Rohypnol (roofies), and Amobarbital. It was clear to detectives that all five deaths were linked.

———

Six months prior to Richard Kelvin's murder, a young man named George informed police he had been kidnapped, drugged, and raped by several people. He told detectives that while hitchhiking, he was picked up by an older man who offered him alcohol in the backseat of his car and enticed him to come to a nearby house to drink with some older women. At the house, the women flirted with him and gave him more alcohol. After some time, he began feeling drowsy and the last thing he remembered was being taken into a bedroom to have sex with one of the women. Just before he blacked out, he realized that the woman was not female, but a transvestite.

George woke up the next day in his own home, but crippled with pain and no recollection of the rest of the night or how he got home. He went to the police to report the incident and agreed to a medical and toxicological test. He had severe lacerations in his anus and his blood contained a significant quantity of Mandrax. It was the same drug that was found in the systems of Richard Kelvin and Mark Langley.

Detectives searched through prior police reports and found many similar stories. There were several other young men that had also been abducted, drugged, and raped.

Mandrax had become a popular recreational drug in the late 1970s, known on the street as "Randy Mandys." It was a date-rape drug. This led the South Australia government to regulate it and several other drugs. After its regulation, every prescription of the drug had a paper trail and police believed their best option was to search for who had access to these drugs.

Detectives took the time to sift through thousands of records of individuals in South Australia that had been prescribed Mandrax. After extensive searches, the name Bevan Spencer von Einem came up.

———

Bevan Spencer von Einem

At first appearance, von Einem seemed normal enough. He was in his late thirties, prematurely gray, worked as an accountant, and still lived with his mother. Detectives questioned von Einem at his workplace and at home without prior notice. They wanted to surprise him and not give him the opportunity to prepare his answers. When asked about his prescriptions, von Einem explained he was an insomniac and had trouble sleeping his entire life. He claimed the prescriptions for Mandrax and Rohypnol were to help him sleep. He flatly denied knowing any of the victims other than Neil Muir.

When asked about his whereabouts on the night Richard Kelvin was kidnapped, he had an answer prepared. He claimed he was home sick with the flu the entire week and his mother could back up his story.

von Einem seemed to have prepared answers for every question, often giving racist comments baselessly suggesting that people like Lebanese, Greek, or Italian immigrants must have committed the murders. When asked point-blank if he had committed the murders, he gave a strange response, telling the detectives,

"No, of course not. That would be unethical."

———

Detectives tracked down the anonymous caller, "Mr. B," who had mentioned von Einem years earlier. He agreed to speak to detectives again on the condition that he could remain anonymous. Mr. B was in his early twenties, which meant he would have been a teenager when he associated with von Einem. He claimed he would ride with von Einem while he drove around Adelaide, picking up young boys on the streets.

The men would offer boys a ride and give them alcohol from a cooler that von Einem always kept in the back seat of his car. After a few drinks, the boys were invited to a party with more alcohol and women. von Einem would then offer the boys what he told them was "NoDoz", a popular caffeine pill at the time. But rather than caffeine, the pills were actually one of his powerful sedatives.

After the boys had passed out from the sedatives, Mr. B claimed von Einem would take the boys to a house owned by two transgender women, where they would be raped by multiple men, often with a bottle. Afterwards, most of them would be released with only a vague recollection of what had happened to them.

Mr. B's explanation was virtually the same as what the young man, George, had told them. Although police were glad to have the information about von Einem, they believed that Mr. B had more involvement than he was admitting. The young man had been careful not to implicate himself, however, and claimed to have witnessed the events, but never participated.

———

In the Fall of 1983, investigators searched von Einem's home he shared with his mother. Although there was no evidence of a murder having happened at the residence, they did find his prescription for Mandrax in his bathroom. He claimed that was the only drug he had, but when police continued their search, several more drugs were found in a duffel bag. Even more were hidden on a secret ledge hidden behind his closet. The drugs were the same that had been found in the bodies of the victims: Noctec, Valium, and Rohypnol. Samples were also taken of von Einem's hair and blood.

On the evening after the search of von Einem's home, detectives parked nearby and watched as a man who would later become known as "Mr. R" visited von Einem. Mr. R was a businessman in Adelaide and a close friend of von Einem. The man remained at the house for several hours.

———

Bevan Spencer von Einem was arrested and charged with the murder of Richard Kelvin on November 3, 1983. Prosecutors believed the link between the drugs found in Richard Kelvin's body and the drugs found in von Einem's home was enough to convict him for that murder. The other four murders would have to wait.

Over the next several months, detectives gathered evidence. Of the 925 fibers found on Richard Kelvin's clothing, 250 of them came from von Einem's bedroom carpet, bedspread, and cardigan sweater. von Einem's hairs were found inside Richard's jeans.

Between December 1978 and August 1983, von Einem had been prescribed 5,873 tablets and capsules of the six different types of sedatives, often filling the prescriptions from three different pharmacists on the same day.

———

Police believed that von Einem murdered all five boys, but he wasn't alone. He had to have had help. Neil Muir had been butchered in such a way that they believed someone with surgery experience was involved. The same experience would have been needed for the surgery that was done to Mark Langley. There were accounts of several people in a car abducting Richard Kelvin, while additional accounts pointed toward several other men involved in the rapes, as well as transgender women.

Investigators searched a building owned by von Einem's associate, Mr. R, in central Adelaide. The entire second floor of the building was vacant, with only a mattress lying on the floor. Police believed this could have been a location they used to rape the young boys.

Mr. R was a gay man that was known to spend his lunch breaks cruising gay areas of Adelaide looking for young men. His roommate was a doctor named Stephen George Woodwards. Woodwards had been accused multiple times of sexual assault, eventually facing charges. Police believed Woodwards could have performed the surgery that was done to Mark Langley.

Although detectives were able to show that von Einem ran in the same circles as these men, they had trouble directly linking them to any of the crimes.

———

With the discovery of the fibers and hairs on Richard Kelvin's clothes, von Einem changed his story. Initially, he had claimed he was sick with the flu for a full week during Richard's disappearance. He even had a prescription filled. Now he claimed he had been driving in the area to get some fish and chips when he encountered Richard Kelvin. He told detectives he struck up a conversation with Richard and the fifteen-year-old boy came with him willingly. He claimed they drove around the city and talked. Richard spoke to him at length about school problems and girlfriend problems. von Einem claimed he then brought Richard back to his home, where they talked some more. He said that at one point he put his arm around Richard, which he explained as the reason that fibers from his cardigan were found on Richard's clothes. He claimed that the carpet fibers on Richard's body were from when he sat on the floor while von Einem played the harp for him. von Einem then explained that he gave Richard $20 for a taxi ride back home and that was the last he had seen of him.

Detectives didn't buy his story for a minute. The fibers from von Einem's carpet and his own hairs were found on the inside of Richard's clothing, not the outside. Also, Richard had died five weeks after he went missing. Any such fibers from the day he went missing would have been gone by that amount of time.

More importantly, von Einem had just admitted that he was the last person to see Richard alive. Despite the evidence against him, von Einem pleaded not-guilty.

Bevan Spencer von Einem's trial started on October 15, 1984. His defense tried to imply that Richard Kelvin was secretly bisexual, which wasn't true, and ultimately didn't make a difference to their case. von Einem was found guilty on November 5 after less than eight hours of deliberation. The conviction came with an automatic life sentence with parole eligibility in twenty-four years. Eight of those years could be taken off for good behavior.

von Einem could conceivably have been released in as little as sixteen years. The Attorney General, however, filed an immediate appeal to lengthen the parole period. As a result, his parole eligibility was extended to thirty-six years.

The first guest to visit von Einem in jail was Mr. R

In the years after von Einem's conviction, detectives searched for evidence to convict von Einem or any accomplices for the additional four murders. A $250,000 reward was offered for information leading to an arrest and over time the reward was gradually increased to $1,000,000, but with no results.

Mr. B continued to provide the prosecution with information claiming that von Einem and Mr. R had made a snuff film of the killing of Alan Barnes. He also told police that von Einem had been involved in the Beaumont Children's disappearance in 1966, as well as the disappearance of two girls from an Australian rules football match in 1973. Of course, the accusations were just Mr. B's word without actual evidence.

Mr. B's sister contacted police and claimed that her brother once told her he had participated in the abduction and murder of a young man in Adelaide. She claimed they threw the body off a bridge. Again, without actual evidence.

By 1990, armed only with circumstantial evidence, prosecutors brought von Einem back to trial for the murders of Alan Barnes and Mark Langley. In a massive blow to the prosecution, much of the evidence presented, however, was deemed inadmissible by the court. In order to avoid a possible acquittal, the charges were eventually dropped.

———

One of the detectives working the case appeared on the television news show "60 Minutes." During the show, he spoke of his desire to break up "the happy family," referring to his belief that there were many more people helping von Einem commit the crimes. He believed there was evidence linking wealthy Adelaide businessmen, politicians, judges, and doctors, all child sex abusers.

Over the next few decades, the case remained the subject of conspiracy theories throughout South Australia. Many people believed to have been involved remain with their identity hidden, while others have been revealed.

————

Mr. R - Known to be a longtime friend of von Einem and visited him in prison multiple times. Police have long suspected him as an accomplice to the murders but were unable to produce evidence.

Dr. Stephen Woodwards - Woodwards refused to answer questions to police. Investigators believed he supplied von Einem with drugs and may have helped butcher the victims, as well as sexually assaulting them.

Denis St Denis - Another of von Einem's longtime friends as well as his hairdresser. Police believe Richard Kelvin was held at St Denis' home while he was tortured and killed.

Mr. B - Although he was careful not to implicate himself when questioned by police, detectives believe he was involved in many of the abductions.

Prudence Firman - A transgender woman who had a sex change in 1982 is believed to have allowed use of her home for abductions in exchange for drugs.

Noel Terrance Brooks - Was believed to have been seen with Peter Stogneff on the day he disappeared.

Derrance Stevenson - A high profile lawyer that was an associate of Alan Barnes. Stevenson dealt heroin from his home and was known for his predilection for young boys. He was murdered by his nineteen-year-old lover, David Szach, just weeks after Alan's murder.

Gino Gambardella - Fled Australia to Italy after several accusations of sexual assault. He's a close friend of both von Einem and Stevenson.

The list of suspected involved parties goes on and on.

Another gay man with an association to von Einem was Trevor Peters. After his death in 2014, his family found a diary as they sifted through his belongings.

Entries in the diary discussed his relationship with von Einem in detail and several others listed above. The diary alleged that von Einem had discussed the abduction of Alan Barnes with his hairdresser, Denis St Denis, and laughed about taking photos of Barnes as he was being held captive.

Another person implicated in the diary was Lewis Turtur. Turtur was well-known as a flamboyant drag queen whose brother was a famous Olympic athlete. When news crews confronted Turtur about his association with von Einem, Turtur admitted his involvement and admitted to abducting boys, but insisted he had nothing to do with the murders.

> "All I know is they came in... he dropped them off at our place, he went home, we let them sleep it off, they left in the morning. I was a stupid fool, wasn't I? Half the time I was drugged out anyway, so I don't really care. I was in my own little world."

Investigators believe there may have been as many as 150 abductions and many more murders throughout the years that have been unreported or unlinked. Although many associates of von Einem, all with a passion for young boys, were believed to have been involved, none have ever been charged.

———

This chapter is a free bonus chapter from True Crime Case Histories: Volume 7

Online Appendix

Visit my website for additional photos and videos pertaining to the cases in this book:

http://TrueCrimeCaseHistories.com/vol3/

THANK YOU!

Thank you for reading this Volume of True Crime Case Histories. I truly hope you enjoyed it. If you did, I would be sincerely grateful if you would take a few minutes to write a review for me on Amazon using the link below.

https://geni.us/TrueCrime3

I'd also like to encourage you to sign-up for my email list for updates, discounts and freebies on future books! I promise I'll make it worth your while with future freebies.

http://truecrimecasehistories.com

And please take a moment and follow me on Amazon.

https://geni.us/TrueCrime

One last thing. As I mentioned previously, many of the stories in this series were suggested to me by readers like you. I like to feature stories that many true crime fans haven't heard of, so if there's a story that you remember from the past that you haven't seen covered by other true crime sources, please send me any details you can remember and I will do my best to research it. Or if you'd like to contact me for any other reason free to email me at:

jasonnealbooks@gmail.com

https://linktr.ee/JasonNeal

Thanks so much,

Jason Neal

More books by Jason Neal

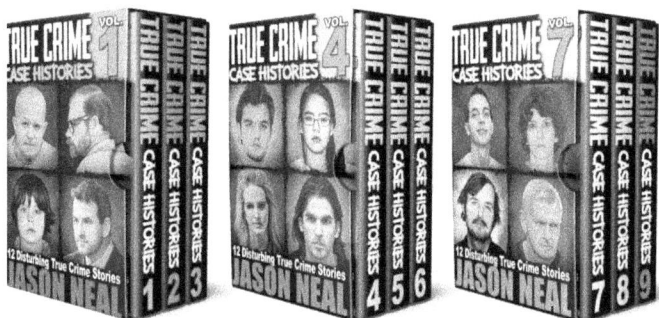

Looking for more?? I am constantly adding new volumes of True Crime Case Histories. The series **can be read in any order**, and all books are available in paperback, hardcover, and audiobook.

Check out the complete series at:

https://amazon.com/author/jason-neal

or

http://jasonnealbooks.com

All Jason Neal books are also available in **AudioBook format at Audible.com.** Enjoy a **Free Audiobook** when you signup for a 30-Day trial using this link:

https://geni.us/AudibleTrueCrime

FREE BONUS EBOOK FOR MY READERS

As my way of saying "Thank you" for downloading, I'm giving away a FREE True Crime e-book I think you'll enjoy.

https://TrueCrimeCaseHistories.com

Just visit the link above to let me know where to send your free book!

ABOUT THE AUTHOR

Jason Neal is a Best-Selling American True Crime Author living in Hawaii with his Turkish-British wife. Jason started his writing career in the late eighties as a music industry publisher and wrote his first true crime collection in 2019.

As a boy growing up in the eighties just south of Seattle, Jason became interested in true crime stories after hearing the news of the Green River Killer so close to his home. Over the subsequent years he would read everything he could get his hands on about true crime and serial killers.

As he approached 50, Jason began to assemble stories of the crimes that have fascinated him most throughout his life. He's especially obsessed by cases solved by sheer luck, amazing police work, and groundbreaking technology like early DNA cases and more recently reverse genealogy.